THE
TREASURY

OF

QUOTES
LYRICS

&

POEMS

THE TREASURY OF QUOTES LYRICS & POEMS

By Dan Clark, CSP, CPAE
New York Times Best Selling Author
Hall of Fame Speaker
University Professor
Gold Record Songwriter
Closet Philosopher

The illiterate of the future are not those who can't read or write, but those who cannot learn, unlearn, relearn, re-wire, re-engineer and re-energize their minds and bodies to take action on what they've relearned — not from long grueling school courses and complicated curriculums, but from short, simple, profound, provocative timeless truths.

IZZARD INK
PUBLISHING

Table of Contents

Foreword

My fascination for researching, writing, and memorizing memorable quotes was created and nurtured by my dear, sweet mother, Ruby Clark. It's been said, 'Wisdom is the gift of the elderly – when an old woman dies an entire library burns to the ground.' True – especially for my mom.

Throughout my life she has continuously fed me a steady diet of golden nuggets of wisdom and elevated my current understanding with quotable quotes.

Consequently, I have become obsessed with writing powerful persuasive paragraphs, one-liners, and thought-provoking songs, where you take an entire story and distill it into three and a half minutes. The "hook" of a catchy chorus line is what makes it a hit, such as: "Thank God for unanswered prayers," "Whiskey for my men - beer for my horses," "How do you like me now?" "Live like you're dying," "It was the sickness that made me well," "In two more days tomorrow's yesterday," "Had I shot you when I met you I'd be out of jail by now, "I gave up smoking, drinking and women last night - and it was the worst fifteen minutes of my entire life."

In a joke, the punch line is what makes the entire joke funny: During a test a kid whispers, 'How close are you to the answer?' His friend replies, 'Two seats away!'

In sports, when the pressure is on, it's the concise truisms that guide your behavior, such as the one my coach Tom Gadd taught, "Sportsmanship is when an athlete walks off the field and you can't tell whether he has won or lost. His hushed dignity, respect for the game, and knowledge that he left it all on the field let him stand tall and be proud."

Yes, we all need and should continuously seek the wisdom of a mentor.

Teacher Verses Mentor

Mentors are different than teachers. Oftentimes teachers confuse teaching with talking. Oftentimes teachers blame their inability to instruct someone as a 'learning disability' when in fact it's a 'learning difference' with a 'teaching disability.'

Of course, I love and honor educators. Teaching is the profession that makes all other professions possible. No one in our world would even have a job if it wasn't for our wonderful teachers. They have dreams for sale in every sense of the word.

However, a mentor is a master teacher, who teaches with the mindset of a coach who understands that the only place from which a person can grow is where he or she is. So, they go where we are physically and emotionally because it is only there where they can gently invite us to learn and improve.

The title 'teacher' sounds academic and sterile as they enforce the letter of the law. Teachers see with eyesight, but 'mentors' see with insight. The title 'mentor' encompasses passion and wisdom. Mentors are emotional and enforce the spirit of the law. Mentors use creativity to cut through the clutter of daily life to reveal the simple truths that empower us.

For example, my mentor, S. Wayne Clark (my dad) forever changed my life when he shared with me the following:

> "You are under no obligation to be the same person you were a year, month, day, or even 15 minutes ago. You have the right to grow. But can only grow when you comprehend sadness gives depth - happiness gives height. Sadness gives roots - Happiness gives branches. Happiness is like a tree going up into the sky, and sadness is like the roots going down into the womb of the earth. The higher a tree grows, the deeper it goes. The bigger the tree, the bigger the roots — simultaneous and in proportion."

Because of the depth of this profound observation, I committed this quote to memory that it might become part of my everyday thought and conversational repertoire.

In fact, after experiencing the incredible impact that it had on me and my attitude during just one day, I also memorized the following seven quotes to add to this understanding so they would become part of my everyday thoughts, which I can share in the flow of every conversation:

> "Improve before you have to; Give before
> you get; Be strong before you need to be."

"An armored-up warrior never has to get ready — he/she stays ready!" - Navy Seal

"The two most important days of your life are the day you were born and the day you find out why." - Mark Twain

"Everybody is a genius. But if you judge a fish by its ability to climb a tree it will spend its entire life believing it is stupid." - Einstein

"Just because my path is different doesn't mean I'm lost."

"The man who views the world at 50 the same way he did at 20 has wasted 30 years of his life."
-   Muhammad Ali

"Life is not measured by the number of breaths we take, but by the moments that take our breathaway." - Maya Angelou

"The most visible creators are those artists whose medium is life itself. The ones who express the inexpressible — without brush, hammer, clay,or guitar. They neither paint nor sculpt. Their medium is being. Whatever their presence touches has increased life. They see and they don't have to draw. They are the artists of being alive." - J. Stone

Foundation

Every physical, mental, and spiritual structure is built on a foundation that either supports and stabilizes it or leads to its demise and destruction. The ability of that structure to withstand every scientific, philosophical, and psychological test and endure for time and all eternity is dependent on the solid, unshakeable strength of that foundation.

For this reason, this collection of Wisdom, Rhymes, Wizardry, 'Clarkisms,' Quotes, Poems and Lyrics rests on one scientifically proven, theological truth:

There is a set of universal laws, irrevocably decreed and set in motion as the foundations of this world, uponwhich all increase, profits and desired outcomes are predicated. When we achieve anything personally or accomplish anything professionally, it is by strict obedience to that law upon which it is predicated. When we obey the law we reap the rewards attached to that law. When we disobey we suffer the specific consequence.

Based on this awareness, this Treasury highlights the Twelve Highest Universal Laws that govern us featured in Dan's bestselling book: The Art of Significance -Achieving The Level Beyond Success.

Law 1

Practice Obedience Beyond Freewill Agency

because Obedience is the first and highest Law of the Universe, by which all other laws, rules and principles are governed, protected, and preserved, knowing that in order for any law to work in our lives, wemust choose to act accordingly.

It is not enough to say I will do my best. We must succeed in doing that which is necessary.

Every day we need to start our day by asking: 'Where am I right now?' Because no matter where you go there you are. A geographic relocation doesn't change much! You must stand up from where you sit and grow healthy and strong from where you are planted. Whenever we book an Uber ride, we are required to enter in our present location. If we lie about where we are, the directions won't work!

Knowledge is power, but knowledge has no heart. Reason leads to conclusions, but it is emotion that leads to action.

We must seek wisdom, not just information. Wisdom is applied knowledge. All the information in the world isn't going to make a person successful. It's like the guy who has three PhDs: one in philosophy, one in psychology, one in sociology. He doesn't have a job but at least he can explain why!

When the precious metal silver is heated up, because each vat of the molten metal responds differently to the same temperature, the artist has but one technique to know when the liquid stands ready for pouring into a beautiful shape. Only when the artist cansee his face reflecting back at him from the silver is it ready to be molded into something more. Whenever we feel the "heat" in a test to see what we are made of, only when we look ourselves in the eye with the "man-in-the-mirror" reflecting back at us are we ready to mold and shape the man we are into the something-more-man that we need to be.

We can't afford to learn just from our own experiences. We must shorten our learning curve and learn from other's mistakes, victories, and defeats. When we know what and why a champion thinks the way he thinks, and how, where and when he prepares, we too can become champions!

In a research project conducted by The Brooks Group, where they reviewed 12,000 face-to-face sales presentations, they discovered that when sales professionals had a specific sales system and step-by-step process they meticulously followed they had a 93% closing rate. Without it, their chances dramatically droppedto 42%.

Don't regret growing older. It is a privilege denied to many; Don't fear death - fear that you never really lived at all; Don't live in the past - it makes you depressed; Don't live in the future - it makes you anxious. Live only in the present - it creates peace.

Every morning make a list of things that make you happy; Then make a list of things you do every day; Compare the lists; Adjust accordingly.

Bottom Line

"To every man, there comes in his lifetime that special moment when he is tapped on theshoulder and offered the chance to do a very special thing, unique to him and fitted to his talents. What a tragedy if that moment finds him unprepared and unqualified for the work which would be his finest hour." - Winston Churchill

"The strongest is never strong enough to be always
the master unless he transforms strengthinto right,
and obedience into duty." - Jean Jacques Rousseau

Invictus

Out of the night that covers me
Black as the pit from pole to pole
I thank whatever Gods may be
For my unconquerable soul

In the fell clutch of circumstance
I have not winced nor cried aloud
Under the bludgeoning of chance
My head is bloody, but unbowed

Beyond this place of wrath and tears,
Looms the horror of the shade
And yet the menace of the years
Finds, and shall find me unafraid

It matters not how strait the gate
How charged with punishments the scroll
I am the master of my fate:
I am the captain of my soul"
- William Ernest Henley

Law 2

Exercise Perseverance Beyond Patience

because there is a difference between temporary defeat and failure; so when plans fail we substitute other plans but do not change our purpose.

Today you've never been this old before, and today you'll never be this young again — so right now, and every right now matters. Which means no matter what your past has been you have a spotless future. You can't always control what happens, but you can always control what happens next.

With his invention of the light bulb, Thomas Edison didn't fail 999 times. The light bulb was an invention with 1,000 steps.

Attitude is everything. When your attitude is right, your abilities will always catch up.

Patience is not always a virtue. Any virtue taken to the extreme can become a vice. Patience allows you to never begin! The higher law is Perseverance, which is patience with a purpose. Patience enables you to live life with a victim mentality of 'whoa me. 'This is the hand I've been dealt and the cross I must bare, so I will mindlessly wait my turn because it's meant to be. Perseverance empowers you to intentionally 'take your turn' and never let what you cannot do interfere with what you can do.

Yes life is hard, but adversity introduces you to yourself, and makes you either bitter or better.

Pain is a signal to grow, not to suffer. Once we learn the lesson the pain is teaching us the pain goes away. Therefore, in life there are no mistakes, only lessons.

The gem cannot be polished without friction, norman perfected without trials.

Healing doesn't mean the damage never existed. It means the damage no longer controls our lives.

What you've been in the past does not make you who you are today as much as what you plan to become in the future makes you who you are today. Your future depends on what you do in the present.

Character is developed in the workshop of our daily lives, practiced in the uneventful, commonplace routine of life, so in the great moments of test and trial, our character can be displayed.

When something is important to you, you will always find a way. When it's not, you will always find an excuse.

People who wonder if the glass is half empty or half full have missed the point. It's refillable! Thinking positively or negatively doesn't fill up the glass — the pouring does. It's easier to act your way into positive thinking than to think your way into positive action. It's not the sugar that makes the tea sweet - it's the stirring. No matter what, you know 'enough' right now and have 'enough' skill right now to do something positive and productive, right now.

Perseverance is adding value to value. We don't have to see the whole staircase to take the first step. We need only see and feel the value of taking the next step, realizing courage is staying one step ahead of fear.

Regardless of whether we are leisurely strolling in the park, competing in the Olympic Games, climbing Mt. Everest, or striving to be significant, one step at a time is good walking, one step at a time is good running, one step at a time is good climbing, one day at a time is good living!

The only thing you are not in charge of is whether you are in charge.

The acronym H.A.L.T.S. is the red flag warning that inhibits perseverance. When you are Hungry, Angry, Lonely, Tired, or Sad, you cannot think clearly, listen intently, feel passionately, or have energy to endure. Replace hunger with nutritious food; replace anger with forgiveness; loneliness with service; tiredness (which makes cowards of us all) with exercise and rest; and sadness with a personal dream.

Exhaustion is acceptable; falling is acceptable; puking is acceptable; crawling is acceptable; blood, sweat and tears are acceptable; heartache and discouragementare acceptable; and whining, complaining, blaming, and quitting are not.

44% of sales professionals quit after the first sales call; 24% quit after the second sales call; 14% quit after the third sales call; 12% quit after the fourth sales call. This means 94% of sales professionals quit by the fourth sales call. Yet 80% of most sales are closed between the 5th and 12th sales calls!

You shouldn't be so quick to claim your limitations when perhaps you've never truly tested them. You never know how strong you are until being strong is the only choice you have - even if it's being strong at only one thing.

What's holding you back? The greatest mistake you can make in life is to continually fear you will make one.

The start is what stops most people; yes, it takes courage to grow up and become who you really are.

When you take a chance on doing just once what others say you can't do, you will never pay attention to their limitations again.

Dependence on another is a perpetual disappointment.

Bottom Line

"Endurance is not just the ability to bear a hard thing, but to turn it into glory." - William Barclay

"All great masters are chiefly distinguished by the power of adding a second, a third, and perhaps a fourth step in a continuous line. Many a man has taken the first step. With every additional step you enhance immensely the value of your first."
—Ralph Waldo Emerson

If

If you can keep your head when all about you are
losing theirs and blaming it on you;
If you can trust yourself when all men doubt you but
make allowance for their doubting too.

If you can wait and not be tired by waiting, or being
lied about, don't deal in lies,
Or being hated don't give way to hating,
And yet don't look too good, nor talk too wise.

If you can dream - and not make dreams your
master, if you can think - and not make thoughts
your aim,
If you can meet with Triumph and Disaster,
And treat those two impostors just the same.

If you can bear to hear the truth you've spoken,
twisted by knaves to make a trap for fools,
Or watch the things you gave your life to, broken,
And stoop and build 'em up with worn out tools.

If you can make one heap of all your winnings, and
risk it on one turn of pitch-and-toss, and lose, and
start again at your beginnings,
And never breathe a word about your loss.

If you can force your heart and nerve and sinew, to
serve your turn long after they are gone, and sohold
on when there is nothing in you,
Except the Will which says to them: Hold on!

If you can talk with crowds and keep your virtue
or walk with Kings - nor lose the common touch,
If neither foes nor loving friends can hurt you,
If all men count with you, but none too much.

If you can fill the unforgiving minute, with sixty
seconds worth of distance run, yours is the Earth
and everything that's in it,
And – which is more - you'll be a Man, my son!"
-    Rudyard Kipling

Law 3

Intentionally Stretch Beyond Change

*because human beings are hardwired
for progress, not to morph into something we
are not, but to become more of who
we already are.*

Under pressure, you don't step up your game - you succumb to the level of your preparation and practice. This means pressure is not something that is naturally there. It's created when you question your own ability. When you know what you've been trained to do, there is never any question. So, if you ever decide to give up, you will quit during practice and not in a game. That's why you train and practice so hard.

To create a culture of excellence and build a winning team, your continuous commitment to personal development must be equal to or greater than your commitment to professional development.

The only place from which people can grow is where they are. To inspire others to reach their full potential in attitude and execution, you must go to where they are physically and emotionally. Only there can you gently invite them to stretch and improve.

Change from the outside in is reactive and creates pressure and stress. Change from the inside out is proactive and creates power, which is not change at all. It is 'stretching' and self-development and continuous personal and organizational improvement - not because it is expected by others, but because it is de- manded of ourselves.

'No pain, no gain' really means 'no heart, no chance.'

Too many hate their jobs and only look forward to Friday instead of Monday. They think they are paid by the hour, when in reality we are paid for the value we bring to that hour. Creating personal value comes when you do what others are not willing to do. No, you don't want to do it either, but you do it any way!

Too many think nobility comes by being superior to some other person, when true nobility comes only in being superior to your previous self by never letting what you cannot do interfere with what you can do, and taking charge of your destiny one moment at a time.

Every time you stay out late; every time you sleep in; every time you miss a workout; every time you don't give 100%… you make it that much easier for someone to beat you - not because he/she is bigger, faster, stronger, smarter - but because you have already beaten yourself.

When you do today what others won't, you will accomplish tomorrow what others can't, turn your stumbling blocks into steppingstones, and join my 'Community of Significance' who realize that while some people spend their entire lives wishing for amazing things they will never get, we focus just on doing amazing things with whatever we have.

The past is gone, the future has not come - all I have is right now to be everything I was born to be. If I spend my time trying to be somebody else, who is going to be me? I will make a lousy somebody else. Today really is the first day of the rest of my life!

Bottom Line

"Don't wish it was easier; wish you were better. If you are not willing to risk the unusual, you will have to settle for the ordinary. The few who do are the envy of the many who only watch. Life responds to deserve and not to need. Formal education will make you a living. Self-education will make you a fortune." – Jim Rohn

"It is not the strongest of the species that survives, nor the most intelligent that survives. It is the one that is most adaptable to change." - Darwin

"Far better is it to dare mighty things, to win glorious triumphs, even though checkered by failure... than to rank with those poor spirits who neither enjoy nor suffer much, because they live in a gray twilight that knows not victory nor defeat."
- Theodore Roosevelt

Law 4

Trust Predictability
Beyond Hope & Faith

*because faith without works is not faith at
all, and consistent repetition of an attitude
and course of action in the pastand present
suggests we can expect it to continue in the
future.*

Too many live their lives hoping to be happy. But
because they only hope, they never really are. They are
waiting for someone to ask them to the senior prom
and have never taken the time to learn how to dance.

Hope is walking through a destructive fire; Faith is
leaping over the fire; Trusting Predictability is learning
from others so you can either avoid the fire or use it in
a positive constructive way to make you and your
circumstances better.

We don't attract who we want. We attract who we are. We attract what we believe we deserve in relationships, work, lifestyle and community.

We don't measure people when they are up – we measure them when they are down. You'll never meet a strong person with a weak past.

The relationships you have with others are only as healthy, trustworthy, reliable, loving, and loyal as you are.

When you put a hard to catch horse in the same field with an easy to catch horse, you usually end up with two hard to catch horses. When you put a sick child in the same room with a healthy child, you usually end up with two sick children. To be disciplined, healthy and significant, you must associate with the disciplined, healthy, and significant.

Wealth flows through you, not to you. Which means you can get anything in life that you want, if you are willing to help enough other people get what they want.

In fiction we find the predictable boring. In real life we find the unpredictable terrifying. Therefore, you can only be unpredictable once.

It's better to have a reliable and predictable enemy than an unpredictable friend — at least we know where we are with them.

Crisis does not make or break the man or woman. It just reveals the true character within. It's not what happens to you that defines who you are. It's what you do with what happens to you that defines who you are.

The bottom-line definition of sales is 'the transference of trust.' This explains why if money is the major topic of conversation, it means the presentation is weak and the relationship is non-existent.

Trust is logical and short term, requiring constant verification where you assess the probabilities of gain and loss, calculate expected utility based on past performance data, and conclude that the person in question will behave in a predictable manner. Distrust is emotional and long term, in that 'I'm not upset that you lied to me, I'm upset that from now on I can't believe you.

Treat me right the first time because I can't guaran- tee you a next time. It's impossible to keep me once you've lost my trust.

If you pursue happiness, it will elude you. But if you focus on your family, the needs of others, your work, meeting new people, and transforming your life from successful to significance, happiness will find you.

Bottom Line

'I fear not the man who has practiced 10,000 kicks once. I fear the man who has practiced one kick 10,000 times.' - Master martial artist Bruce Lee

"Animals are reliable, many full of love, truein their affections, predictable in their actions, grateful and loyal. Difficult standards for people to live up to." - Alfred Montaper

"When we treat a man as he is, we make him worse than he is; but when we treat him as if he is already what he potentially could be, he becomes what he should be." - Goethe

"Our deepest fear is not that we are inadequate. Our deepest fear is that we are powerful beyond measure. It is our Light, not our Darkness, that most frightens us. You are a child of God. Your playing small does not serve the world. There is nothing enlightened about shrinking so that other people won't feel insecure about you. We were born to manifest the glory of God that is within us." - Marianne Williamson

Law 5

Know The Whole Truth Beyond Believing What You Think

because behind every reality is a specific cause. Often the cause is so far removed from the effect that the circumstance canbe explained only as luck or coincidence. But everything in life is capable of proof by seeking Whole Truth. The entire and complete truth is what sets us free.

Some things are true whether you believe them or not; everybody is entitled to an opinion, but nobody is entitled to the wrong facts; and you shouldn't believe everything you think.

Believing is nothing more than a badge pinned on your lapel. Knowing is a deep and abiding unshakeable conviction in your spirit.

It's much better not to know than to have answers that are wrong. Those afraid of the universe as it really is, will prefer the fleeting comforts of superstition. They avoid rather than confront the world. But those with the courage to explore the structure of the universe, even where it differs profoundly from their wishesand prejudices, will penetrate its deepest mysteries.

You can have understanding without knowledge but having knowledge without understanding is worthless.

Understanding our knowledge is the 'why' to action.

Don't just hear me out - listen. Don't just understand what I'm saying - I yearn to be understood.

Bottom Line

"Cities, like San Francisco, are literary art. Every block is a short story, every hill a novel, every home a poem, every dweller within immortal. That is the whole truth." - William Saroyan

"Learning which thou gets by thy own observation and experience from looking over the wall and going beyond the map, is far beyond that which thou gets by precept; as the knowledge of a traveler exceeds that which is got by reading." - Thomas Kempis

"The man who has a certain religious belief and fears to discuss it, lest it may be proved wrong, is not loyal to his belief, he has but a coward's faithfulness to his prejudices. If he were a lover of truth, he would be willing at any moment to surrender his belief for a higher, better, and truer faith." - William George Jordan

Law 6

Focus On Winning Beyond Team

because individual hustle, sacrifice, willingness to prepare to win, organizational unity, and execution are all driven by purpose and achieving desired results.

There is a difference between training to fight and training to win. And I always win. Either I win or I learn.

Wanting to win doesn't make you a winner - refusing to lose does.

You know you're a champion when losing hurts worse than winning feels good.

There is nothing more insignificant than the halftime score.

Success is never final. Failure is never fatal. You never lose if you always learn. So, you can't quit - it's a league rule.

If you are not training and pushing yourself to your ultimate capacity and potential as a human being, someone else, somewhere else, is. When you meet him, he will win.

Teamwork is the complete conviction that nobody can get there unless everybody gets there.

When the water in the lake goes up, all the boats rise together.

Teams function as a musical ensemble - if you are an oboe player, you don't give up being the very best oboe player to be in the orchestra - you simply need to learn to play as part of an ensemble.

Teamwork is like jazz music - you must know when it's your turn to solo, and your turn to accompany.

Teams are only a reflection of the people on the team. When enough of the people think and act a like a culture is naturally created.

Culture is formed and maintained by the reason you exist as an enterprise and is the primary driving force of performance. The culture at Southwest

Airlines puts them into the customer experience business. They just happen to be an airline.

When we have under-p erforming teams it's because we have under-performing coaches, leaders, and managers who allow and enable a mediocre culture.

Bottom Line

"Winning isn't something that happens suddenly on the field when the whistle blows and the crowds roar. Winning is something that builds physically and mentally every day that you train and every night that you dream." - Emmitt Smith

"The goal is not to do business with everybody who wants what you have. The goal is to only do business with those who believe what you believe, so they choose you, not just somebody who does what you do." - Simon Sinek

"Winning isn't a sometime thing, it's an all-the-time thing. Winning is a habit. Unfortunately, so is losing. Therefore, I firmly believe that any man's finest hour, the greatest fulfillment of all that he holds dear, is that moment whenhe has worked his heart out in a good cause and lies exhausted on the field of battle - victorious." - Coach Vince Lombardi

Dan Clark

Law 7

Do Right Beyond Seeking To Be The Best

because great is not always good enough, and best is only relevant depending on what you are comparing it with.

The main thing is to make the main thing the main thing.

Everybody born into the world comes with an inherent ability to discern truth from error and determine right from wrong. We commonly call this natural intuitive ability our 'conscience.' This means our conscience will never fail us. Only our desire to follow it decreases as we continue to do the wrong thing.

It's better to prepare and prevent than to repair and repent.

It's better to build a fence at the edge of the cliff than to park an ambulance at its base.

If I win a tournament with a score of 108 for 18 holes, this does not mean I am great. It only means I am the best of the worst golfers on the planet who shot 112 for 18 holes!

When the things you think about are different than the things you do, you will never be happy.

Bottom Line

"Place me behind prison walls - walls of stone ever so high, ever so thick, reaching ever so farin the ground - there is a possibility that in some way or another I may be able to escape. But stand me on that floor and draw a chalk line around me and have me give my word of honor never to cross it. Can I get out of that circle? No, never! I'd die first!" - Karl Maeser

"I never had a policy; I have just tried to do the right thing to the very best of my ability each and every day." - Abraham Lincoln

"It is not the critic who counts; not the man who points out how the strong man stumbles, or where the doer of deeds could have done them better. The credit belongs to the man who is actually in the arena, whose faceis marred by dust and sweat and blood; who strives valiantly; who errs, who comes short and again, because there is no effort without error and shortcoming; but who does actually strive to do the deeds; who knowsgreat enthusiasms, the great devotions; who spends himself in a worthy cause; who at the best knows in the end the triumph of high achievement, and who at the worst, if he fails, at least fails while daring greatly, so that his place shall never be with those cold and timid souls who neither know victory nor defeat." - Theodore Roosevelt

Law 8

Experience Harmony
Beyond Forcing Balance

*because you see things as you are - not as they
are. When you get yourself right, the world is
right.*

Don't let what you cannot do interfere with what you
can do.

We don't see things as they are - we see things as we
are. If two people are watching the same snowstorm,
and one negatively complains, 'what a horrible day,'
while the other excitedly exclaim, 'what a wonderful
day,' the weather did not change.

Successful people get what they think they want at the
moment, because they begin with the 'end in mind,'
which creates a limiting belief focused on arriving at a
destination that's impressive, doing their best to
manage people, and rewarding results. Significant

individuals want what they get, by beginning with the 'whyin mind,' which invites them to focus on enjoying thejourney that's important, manage expectations and reward effort.

There are only twelve notes in music. On a piano keyboard there are seven white notes. Five black notes. A total of twelve notes constitute an octave that repeats itself every twelve notes. Every song ever written in any language, in every genre including classical, jazz, rock and roll, R&B, country, opera and electronically synthesized dance jams, was written with the same twelve notes. The only difference between one song and another is the order in which the twelve notes fall, and the timing and spacing between them.

So, what's the difference between a hit songwriter and a lousy songwriter - they have access to the same twelve notes? What's the difference between an astute and visionary banker and a narrow-minded mediocre banker - they have access to the same interest rates and economy? What's the difference between a successful person who gets what he/she wants, and a significant individual who wants what he/she gets? The answer is the same for all: Passion, Creativity, and Imagination.

'Multi-taskers' are simply lousy at a lot of things. It is more effective and efficient to be a 'juggler,' knowing you can only control the ball in your hand. Once you have tossed up the ball you have relinquished control, eliminating any reason to worry, which saves your energy until you catch it again to influence its performance.

Those who transform themselves and their organizations from successful to significant don't just converse-they connect; they don't just see - they feel; they don't just hear - they listen; they don't just have sex - they make passionate love; they don't just think - they believe; they don't just read - they read between the lines. They do more than exist - they truly live!

When you identify yourself in terms of what you do instead of who you are, you become a human doing instead of a human being, which is unacceptable when significance is really what you seek.

There is a giant difference between being depressed and being disappointed - a huge difference between being depressed and being discouraged. Yes, there are people (loved ones and friends) who have a chemical imbalance, who need non-judgmental friendship and our unconditional love, and who need medication prescribed by their physician. However, most people who say they are depressed are not depressed. They are just flippantly and irresponsibly using the word as a popular catchall phrase to describe their disappointment and discouragement.

They have suffered the loss of a loved one, gone through a devastating divorce or the loss of a job, but they are not depressed! They don't have a chemical imbalance like schizophrenia and bipolar disorder and don't need or require medication! Depression medication flattens out one's emotions, eliminating the highs and lows, which numbs and nullifiesone's natural human spirit of resiliency.

When you are disappointed or discouraged you simply need to associate with loved ones and friends who will remind you that if you get knocked down seven times, get up eight.

Circumstances have no power to destroy your dreams. You do not stop dreaming because you are old - you grow old because you stop dreaming. Your dreams either live in your mind and heart, or they die there - it is your choice.

Bottom Line

"Harmony is the analogy of contrary and of similar elements of tone, of color and of line, conditioned by the dominate key, and under the influence of a particular light, in gay, calm. or sad combinations." - George Seurat

"I was part of that strange race of people aptly described as spending their lives doing things they detest, to make money they don't want, to buy things they don't need, to impress people they dislike." - Emile Gauvreau

"Whatever is true, honorable, right, pure, lovely, of good repute, virtuous, excellent and worthy of praise, seek after these things." - Philippians 4:8

Law 9

Accept Others Beyond Judging Them

because to be fully seen by somebody and be loved anyhow is the most miraculous outcome of our human experience.

Every time a man is tempted to react in the same old way, he must ask himself if he wants to be a prisoner of the past or a pioneer of the future. The answer is only found in the place inside him where nothing is impossible. For only there can he begin to become everything he was born to be and the source of inspiration for everyone who knows him.

Every man's heart one day beats its final beat and his lungs breathe their final breath. And if what that man did in his life makes the blood pulse through the body of others and makes them believe deeper in something that's larger than life, then his essence and his spirit, will be immortalized by the loyalty and memory of those who honor him, and who carry on the inspired legacy he created and left behind.

You cannot exceed your potential. You and someone else have just misjudged it.

Whenever you are tempted to sell your soul and give up what you want most for what you think you want at the moment, think like a songwriter thinks. Songwriters want a platinum selling record, which means we sell one million copies. What keeps us strong enough to resist popular demand and stay true to the music we feel inspired to write is the reality that there are 300 million people in America. We can literally tick off 299 million and still go platinum!

Discipline is to teach, not to punish. You cannot increase a person's performance by making that person feel worse. Humiliation immobilizes our behavior.

Miserable being finds other miserable being - then they are happy.

A broken clock is right twice a day. Never give up on anyone - especially yourself.

Bottom Line

"Acceptance is not excusing someone from the consequences of obedience. It is separating the person from the performance and loving him or her into obedience." - Samuel W. Clark, Jr.

"Do not forget to entertain strangers, for byso doing some people have entertained angels without knowing it." - Hebrews 13 Bible

Imagine

Imagine there's no heaven
It's easy if you try
No hell below us
Above us only sky
Imagine all the people
living for today

Imagine there's no countries
It isn't hard to do
Nothing to kill or die for
And no religion too

Imagine all the people
living life in peace
You may say I'm a dreamer
But I'm not the only one

I hope someday you'll join us
And the world will be as one
Imagine no possessions
I wonder if you can

No need for greed or hunger
A brotherhood of man
Imagine all the people
sharing all the world

You may say I'm a dreamer
But I'm not the only one
I hope someday you'll join us
And the world will be as one.
- John Lennon

Law 10

Love And Be Needed Beyond Romanced And Used

because the purpose of life is not to be happy but to matter, to be productive, to be useful - to make a difference in the world.

Love is a commitment, not a way of feeling. Romance is not love. Romance comes from a Greek word that means erotic. If I love you because you're beautiful, that's romance. If you're beautiful because I love you, that's real love - a value creating love that inspires you to become the best you can be.

We don't attract who we want. We attract who we are. Which means we should make a list of things that we deserve in our personal development, health and fitness, intimate relationships, and financial freedom. Then make a listof things we do every day. Compare the lists. Adjust accordingly.

Through the Law of Attraction, you are not looking for someone perfect, you are looking for someonewho is perfect for you, so when you are apart you say, 'I like me best when I'm with you I want to see you again.'

Never measure yourself by what you have accomplished but rather by what you should have accomplished with your abilities.

When you work to leave behind a legacy of love and service, happiness will take care of itself. Remember, caring kindness and leaving your family, friends, and co-workers in better shape than you found them is something the blind can see and the deaf can clearly hear.

If money becomes the topic of conversation, it means the presentation is weak and the relationship is non-existent.

Finding Your 'Soul Mate'

Contrary to pop culture, perpetuated by constant tabloid sensationalism of Hollywood love, finding your "Soul Mate" is not a reality. In the original definition, he/she does not exist.

It is an ancient myth introduced to the world in The Symposium: a philosophical text by Greek philosopher Plato dated c. 385–380 BC, wherein he examines love in a series of speeches by men attending a symposium or drinking party (a boy's night out!).

Make no mistake: I am not suggesting that a soul mate wanders the earth waiting for you. This myth, rooted in ancient Greek mythology, and epitomizing self-centered, narcissistic thinking, is a major destroyer of relationships. As presented in Plato's Symposium, the myth holds that humans had four arms, four legs, and a single head made of two faces.

Because Zeus feared their power, he split them all in half, resulting in a perpetual ache of separation and a longing to regain the completeness by finding one's missing half to recreate the whole. Although harmless terms like "my better half" and "counterpart"evolved from this thinking, another human being was not created just to satisfy your needs or my needs,just to make us feel complete in our "humanness" and become everything we were born to be. We were not 'split-apart' and exiled by the gods to spend our entire lives searching for our missing Mr., Ms. Right/ better half to make us whole.

Soul Mates Are Not
Born - They Are Made

Although it's not possible to be a Soul Mate, becoming someone's Soul Mate is still an extraordinary romantic experience that is worth pursuing, where you share your devotion to the love of your life, promising:

'I will care for you physically and emotionally, and give my whole heart to you, telling and showing you every day, anytime, anywhere, anyway I can, that I love you; constantly yearning to spend more time together gazing into your mesmerizing eyes, feeling the warmth of your infectious smile, and hearing your soft, sweet, soothing, reassuring voice that inspires me to be everything I was born to be; never wanting to go anywhere without you; never caring what other people think about the two of us; and being there for you no matter what, knowing love is the world, the world is love, and you are the world to me.'

Bottom Line

"The individual's most vital need is to prove his worth, and this usually means an insatiable hunger for action wherein he develops and employs his capacities and talents through love, admiration, and genuine interest in the life of another." - Eric Hoffer

"Your 'yes' means nothing if you can't say 'no.' There can be no commitment if there is no choice." - Peter Block

"I find it strange that we buy things we don't need with money we don't have to impress people we don't like. There's a reason why certain people from our past didn't make it into our future." - Dave Ramsey

Law 11

Establish Covenants Beyond Making Commitments

because the lives of both the giver and the receiver of service are positively and simultaneously transformed.

A Commitment is a two-way contract born out of suspicion. You make a list of your responsibilities and I make a list of my responsibilities. You hold me accountable and I hold you accountable. If either one ofus violate any one of the line-item responsibilities, thecommitment contract is broken and void.

A Covenant is a one-way promise born out of love and respect. No matter what you say or whether you keep your word and honor our commitment contract, I will remain the same ethical human being full of unshakable integrity, who will never violate any line item in our contractual agreement regardless of how you treat me.

I don't love and respect you as a human being be- cause of what you have done or who you are. I love and respect you because of who I am, knowing those wrapped up in themselves make a small package.

The Constitution of the United States was never meant to prevent people from praying – its declared purpose was to protect our freedom to pray.

Religion is for those who are afraid to go to hell, and spirituality is for those of us who have already been there.

We are more than mere mortal beings, living on a small planet, for a short season.

Bottom Line

"Do what you can, with what you can, whereyou are." - Theodore Roosevelt

The Soldier

"It is the Soldier, not the minister, who has given us freedom of religion.

It is the Soldier, not the reporter, who has given us freedom of the press.

It is the Soldier, not the poet who has given us freedom of speech.

It is the Soldier, not the campus organizer, who has given us freedom to protest.

It is the Soldier, not the lawyer who has given us the right to a fair trial.

It is the Soldier, not the politician who has given us the right to vote.

It is the Soldier, who salutes the flag, who serves beneath the flag, and whose coffin is draped by the flag, who allows the protesterto burn the flag." - Charles Michael Province

"From whence shall we expect the approachof danger? Shall some trans-Atlantic military giant step the earth and crush us at a blow? Never. All the armies of Europe and Asia couldnot by force take a drink from the Ohio River or make a track on the Blue Ridge in the trial of a thousand years. No, if

destruction be our lot we must ourselves be its
author and finisher. As a nation of free men we will
live forever or die by suicide." – Abraham Lincoln

Law 12

Forgive Beyond Apologizing

because most of the difficulties in which we find ourselves are of our own making; because failure is a state of mind and something we can control; because failure is an event, not a person; and because we will recognize our own weaknesses in others and therefore, cut them some slack.

Forgiveness is at the heart and soul of life and love. Remaining angry is like drinking poison and expecting the other person to die.

Holding a grudge is like being stung to death by a single bee.

Never mix bad words with your bad mood.

Forgiveness is not an occasional act but a constant attitude of 'thank you for that experience.'

Forgiveness is me giving up my right to hurt you for hurting me, which is the greatest manifestation of love.

I think it is intriguing that people find it far easier to forgive others for being wrong than for being right.

Forgiveness is the ultimate expression of love.

What you've been in the past does not make you who you are today as much as what you plan to become in the future makes you who you are today.

Repentance takes as long as it takes for you to say, 'I'm going to change' - and mean it.

A broken clock is right twice a day! Never give up on anybody - especially yourself.

Bottom Line

"Sometimes the more chances you give the more respect you lose. Your standards begin to be ignored when you let people get comfortable in knowing that another chance will always exist. They start to depend on your forgiveness. That's why I am no longer a slave to apologies. I'm not saying that you have to be afraid to lose me. What I'm saying is I'm not afraid to walk away." - Trent Shelton

"A man convinced against his will, is of the same opinion still. It is only with the heartthat one can see rightly; what is essential is invisible to the eye."
- Benjamin Franklin

"We are all on a lifelong journey and the coreof its meaning is found in the three powerful resources we always have available to us: love, prayer, and forgiveness. People fall in love because of chemistry, passion, kindness, and respect. People stay in love because of gratitude, service and forgiveness; Humanity is never so beautiful as when praying for forgiveness; the most tender part of love is forgiveness - one forgives to the degree that one loves - forgiveness is the final form of love."
    -    H. Jackson Brown

Motivational Clarkisms

'Clark Credo'

(Copyright Dan Clark 1985)

I'm smart, talented, and I never say never.
I'm wanted, important, lovable,capable
and I can succeed.

I'm a good athlete, I love music
and I get good grades in school.

The only person I need to be better than is
the person I was yesterday.

So, I never say 'I can't' - I always say 'I can, I
will.'

If I fall or get knocked down
I just get back up and go again.

If I spill or make a mistake, I learn why,
clean it up, and say 'no big deal.'

I love God and He loves me, so I always
treat others as they want to be treated. So
everyone leaves me saying, 'I like me best
when I'm with you. I want to see you again.'

It takes rare courage to leap into an abyss, whether for the thrill of adventure or to dispense with a situation that no longer works. It's easier to hesitate, holding on to the familiar, clinging to people, positions, programs, and possessions that are no longer sustaining, because we fear the unknown. We seek a renaissance of spirit, a return to understanding that being is more important than having, and yet we lose our vitalityby resisting the very steps that could help us create a dynamic and fulfilling life.

When we minimize our hope for success and maximize the effort required to become significant, by focusing not on what's impressive, but on what's important, we see that if the things we think about are different than the things we do we will never be happy.

When you do the things you need to do when you need to do them, you will be able to do the things youwant to do when you want to do them.

Decide to get up thirty minutes earlier than usual in the morning. Do this for a year, and you will add 7.5 days to your waking world. It's better to wear out than to rust out.

If you don't know what direction to take, you haven't acknowledged where you are. You have to see who you are and say what you are, before you can leave where you are and go where you want to be.

When you choose not to continuously train and push yourself to your ultimate capacity and potential as a human being, someone else, somewhere else, will. When you meet him, he will win.

You've got to have a dream. If you don't have a dream how are you going to make a dream come true? When you lose your dreams you die. That's why we have so many people walking the halls of life who are dead and they don't even know it.

Too many drag their dreams down to the level of their income, when we should be using our passion, creativity, imagination, and work ethic to elevate our in- come up to the level of our dreams.

Observational Clarkisms

You cannot get back on your feet until you first get up off your butt.

Working at an unemployment office has to be a tense job – knowing if you get fired you still have to come in the next day.

Anybody who can do at age 65 what he was doing at 25, wasn't doing much at 25.

My friend is addicted to brake fluid but says he can stop anytime he wants.

Marry a short gal and keep your guns on the top shelf. She still might get ya, but you'll hear her dragging the chair across the floor.

Sportscasters in the 'New NFL': "It's not his knee – it appears his feelings have been hurt and the refs have called the new 15 yard 'butt hurt' penalty. The psychologist is attending to him on the field now."

There is a giant difference between inspiration and motivation. Inspiration affects attitude - the way we think. Motivation affects behavior - the way we act. No one person can motivate another person. We can only inspire others to want to motivate themselves.

You cannot discipline the wrong person to do the right thing. There is no right way to do something wrong.

You must learn to do something exactly right slowly before you can learn to do it exactly right quickly.

Don't get discouraged; it is often the last key in the bunch that opens the lock.

The early bird gets the worm, but the second mouse gets the cheese.

You must stretch before you can strengthen, and all the strengthening occurs in the area past the point of discomfort.

What you are afraid to do is a clear indicator of the next thing you need to do.

Everyone dies, but not everyone truly lives. Dream big. When you lose your dreams, you die. So many people walk dead through the halls of life, and they don't even know it.

Dreams come one or two sizes too big so we can grow into them.

If you don't have a dream, how are you going to make a dream come true?

Circumstances never destroy dreams. Dreams live in your mind and heart. Only there can they die.

You are the message. Some people would rather be popular for the moment than respected for a lifetime. Popularity is other people liking you. Happiness is you liking yourself.

Our business in life is not to get ahead of others, but to get ahead of ourselves—to break our own records and to improve our tomorrow through the lessons of yesterday and the actions of today.

Learning is a process we can't skip. Doing is a process of proving that it was worth learning. Start by doing what's necessary; then do what's possible, and suddenly you are doing the impossible.

Quality of life means more than new furniture. The quality of our judgment precisely determines the quality of life.

We do not stop playing because we are old - we grow old because we stop playing.

Reality Clarkisms

We ultimately have no choice but to feel what we are feeling. Authenticity only comes when we compare ourselves with ourselves. The meaning of success and failure emerges only in comparison to something or someone else.

The one-eyed man is king in the land of the blind.

Anorexia and bulimia are not eating disorders; they are not behavioral and have nothing to do with food. A young woman alone on an island with no fashion magazines to look at and no one else around to compare herself against would not know if she was tall or short, skinny, or overweight. She would simply be her real, beautiful, unique self. She would know that 'God don't make no junk!'

You don't have to be positive; you just have to be yourself. But being yourself is a choice, so you should be positive.

We can do only what we think we can do. We can be only what we think we can be. We can have only what we think we can have. What we do, what we are, and what we have all depend upon what we think.

Inspirational Clarkisms

Most of the time, peak performance - taking ourselves to the next level, stretching and becoming everything we were born to be - is inspired only from without until we see it, want it, buy into it, and own it to the degree that it comes from within.

It has been said, 'There are no heroes - only ordinary men and women caught in extraordinary circumstance who place service before self.'

It's also been said that you can't lead where you won't go, and you can't teach what you don't know. I agree, and therefore I don't necessarily respect and follow someone just because he practices what he preaches. Inspiring people preach only what they practice. Inspiration implies that you know something and do something with what you know.

Webster defines a hero as 'a mythological or legendary figure often of divine descent endowed with great strength or ability; an illustrious warrior; a man or woman admired for achievements and noble qualities; one that shows superior courage; the central figure in an event, period, or movement who is the object of extreme devotion; someone's idol; a role model leading by example, inspiring with character, facing all fear, self-sacrificing and exhibiting or marked by daring.'

If you are not rich, notice how you make yourself poor. We do not live to make money; we make money to fully live.

Quality of life is more than new furniture.

We must see who we are and say who we are before we can be who we are.

It's harder to find right answers to the wrong questions than to ask the right questions. And sometimes we need to question the answers!

Success in life is not determined by our abilities; it is determined by our choices. Choices are made based on correct knowledge (truth), correct attitude (what, when, and why we act on knowledge), correct perspective (how knowledge and attitude interface to help us make sense of each situation we encounter), and unquenchable curiosity (relentless questioning of 'if ' and then 'what,' with a cause-and-effect analysis and drive to seek out the best available data to unveil the grandest possibilities).

Success is never final. Charles H. Duell, commissioner of the U.S. Office of Patents said, "Everything that can be invented has been invented." That was 1899. In

1962, a Decca Recording Company executive rejected the Beatles, stating, "I don't like their sound, and guitar music is on the way out."

Real success, self-fulfillment, and peace of mind can only come through living on purpose with someone to love, something to do, and someplace to go in order to feel wanted, important, loved, and capable.

Whatever is sufficient to get us to this point is insufficient to get us further.

Computer memory is getting so powerful that it could eventually hold grudges! In our high-tech world we must seek more truth and then apply it with high touch. High tech is the hardware, mainframe, hard drive, letter-of-the-law side of success where the answers are 100 percent accurate but totally useless. High touch is the software, spirit-of-the-law, intangible qualities side of success where the emotional application of the high-tech knowledge creates wisdom, empathy, compassion, urgency, and action.

Common sense is no longer common. Neither is common courtesy or common knowledge.

Our initial success in life is about saying "yes," but significance and balance are usually about saying "no."

Competition is good, healthy, productive; comparison is destructive. Knowing the difference between competition and comparison is paramount. Comparing brings arrogance, disappointment, and discouragement - and all three are bad.

Competition can bring disappointment, but that's okay - you learn more from failure than success. Success and failure mean nothing by themselves. The meaning of both emerges only in comparison to something or someone else, and this is bad.

Giving half effort doesn't get you half results - it gets you no results.

Unless you try something beyond what you have mastered, you will never grow.

It's not how much you make, but how much you spend - nickels make dollars.

We get what we inspect, not what we expect.

Knowledge is awareness of the fact that fire will burn - wisdom is remembrance.

Clear conscience with pure joy comes only when we choose to fill our minds with truth, fill our hearts with love, and fill our lives with service.

What you are today is the result of what you have thought up to this moment. What you will be tomorrow depends upon the thoughts you think from now on.

Always have family prayer - the family that prays together stays together.

It's not where you serve but how you serve that matters.

Pay a full 10 percent tithe, seek for the Spirit, and stay true to you!

Leadership Clarkisms

The purpose of a leader is to grow more leaders who believe what you believe - not generate more followers. When everybody on the team and in the organization shares common beliefs, winning becomes personal and increased productivity occurs because accountability is self-audited and peer administered.

Standing in the front of a room and calling yourself a leader no more makes you a leader than standing in the middle of a garage makes you a truck!

Anyone who has had the privilege of living a magnificent life filled with extraordinary people and 'Significant Emotional Events' has no right to keep it to himself. He has been tapped out as a thought leader and divinely mentored in his philosophy and understanding of the universe with a calling to show the world that the beliefs and actions of one person, multiplied by the actions of many, can illuminate a biggerpicture, reshape a culture, and empower an entire organization to achieve the level beyond success.

For these reasons, leadership at the lowest level isabout presence, programs, and people; leadership at the highest level is about passion, principles and people. To be an effective manager requires character. To be an effective leader requires credibility. To be inspirational in another person's life requires both character and credibility.

Leadership is an analog job in a digital world. Leaders have courage to adjust mistakes, vision to welcome change, and confidence to stay out of step when everyone else is marching to the wrong tune.

We rise higher and see farther when we stand on the strong shoulders of those who have gone before us and those who continually support us and follow our lead.

Many powerful people leading major organizations and teaching in prestigious educational institutions know the price of everything and the value of nothing; they don't know what they're talking about and make us feel it is our fault. They don't know that they don't know.

A celebrity is a big name; a hero is a big person. The masses define celebrities, but heroes define themselves. Heroes are successful because they are willingto do what others are not willing to do. They do not want to do the hard things in life, either, but theydo them anyway. They understand that courage is the mastery — not the absence of fear.

When everybody thinks alike, nobody thinks very much.

Growth is good, but growth without good growth is no growth.

People first, mission always. You recruit the individual, but you must retain the family.

We enter the armed forces to serve our country, but we fight for our teammates, for each other, for our buddies fighting beside us.

L.E.A.D.E.R.S.H.I.P.:

- Loyalty: to total honesty, God, church, family, righteous friends, country, religious freedom, and every good, clean, positive, productive thing on earth.

- Ethics: knowing hard work pays - a code of conductto always do the right thing simply because it's the right thing to do.

- Ambition: self-starter, relentlessly seeking to know more, be more, and do more today than you did yesterday.

- Duty: to God and to family and family values - to neighbors and community — to country and always voting for the right candidates.

- Excellence in all you do: knowing it's not enough to say 'I will do my best.' You must succeed in doing thatwhich is necessary.

- Respect: for yourself — your mind, body, and spirit - for property, authority and for others.

- Service before self: being empathetic and sensitive to the physical and emotional needs of others and putting their needs before your own.

- Honor: always using your freewill agency to choose obedience - keeping your commitments and promises – establishing your handshake as a signed contract.

- Integrity: always keeping your covenants - remaining the same hard working, character-based person onstage in public as you are off stage in private regardless of how you are treated or the temptations around you.

- Personal Courage: being scared to death and saddling up anyway - facing your fears and running towardsthe sound of the guns.

The Twelve Values of the Boy Scouts of America:

- Trustworthy – always telling the truth, keeping every   commitment and promise with integrity.
- Loyal to those who are not present - refusing to gossip and always defending irrefutable truths.
- Helpful - doing things for others without reward.
- Friendly - to all because there is strength in diversity.
- Courteous - polite to everyone of any age or position.
- Kind - knowing there is strength in being gentle andtreating others as we want to be treated.
- Obedient - to the 'family rules' and laws of the country.
- Cheerful - positively approaching every day with gratitude while striving to make others

happy.
- Thrifty - carefully using time and conserving natural resources and saving for a 'rainy day.'
- Brave - courageous to always stand for what is right.
- Clean - keeping body and mind fit and pure, and home and community spotless.
- Reverent toward the sacred sanctity of life, acknowledging God, respecting the beliefs of others.

Relationship Clarkisms

We resent in others what we don't like about ourselves. Therefore, we must be the change and improvement we seek in our relationships at home and at work. When we stop growing, we put others down out of insecurity to make ourselves feel better about whowe are. Remember, green things keep growing - ripe things go rotten.

If someone says something unkind about me, I must live so that no one will believe it.

If I was accused of being a spiritual, religious, honest, ethical man of God, would they have enough evidence to convict me?

You can't discipline the wrong person to do the right thing. There is no right way to do something wrong.

I've learned that silent company is often more healing than words of advice. 'I didn't know how to fix the doll, I just stayed to help her cry.'

There are only twenty-four hours in a day, and we can't do two things at once. If we say yes to the positive instead of worrying about how to say no to the negative, we won't have time to be negative. Our positives will say no for us. Instead of telling others what they can't do, we should focus on the positive and show them what they can do.

A best friend is one who brings out the best in you.

Failure is an event, not a person. Therefore, praise in public and criticize in private.

Don't expect others to listen to your advice while ignoring your example. I'd rather see a sermon than hear one any day. I'd rather you would walk with me than merely point the way.

Always seek to bless, not impress. Use your wit to amuse, not to abuse.

What you say is exactly what you intend to say.

There are none so self-righteous as the newly converted.

Relationship Selling is everybody's business. Customer service is not a department - it's an attitude. Customers are not outsiders, but a part of the company. Customers do not interrupt the company's work; they are the purpose for it.

Reflective Clarkisms

If at first you don't succeed, then skydiving is probably not for you!

The things we hate to hear the most are usually the things we need to hear the most.

There's no lesson in the second kick of a donkey.

Do not make easy hard. We never lose if we always learn.

Do one thing every day that scares you.

Surround yourself with light; it brightens you and everything you're about.

If you do the things you need to do when you need to do them, you will be able to do the things you want to do when you want to do them.

When we set high expectations and work hard to meet them, we call it accomplishment. We had to come early, study more, and stay late; we had to withstand temptation and take the high road, but it was worth it. However, when we set low expectations and allow our behavior to slide down to meet them, we call it rationalization. Rationalization kills our families, neighborhoods, and schools and can destroy the world.

The person with big dreams, passion, and desire is more powerful than the person with all the facts. We should never drag our dreams down to the level of our income - we should elevate our income up to the level of our dreams.

Good, effective communication is more than two people taking turns talking. Stop, make eye contact, understand, and respond. Don't just hear - listen!

Imagination is the strongest nation on earth.

It's hard to describe the ocean to a land-based creature, and ice to a summer bug.

If you find life is empty, try putting something into it. Kindness is the language the deaf can hear and the blind can see.

Too often we forget that you can surgically remove the stripes from a tiger, and it's still a tiger.

The mountain seems high only from the valley.

Being burned out means that you were once lit! To rekindle the flame, focus on purposes instead of just setting goals.

Failure is the opportunity to begin again with more knowledge.

Some men have thousands of excuses why they cannot do what they want, when all they need is one reason why they can.

Passion will ensure success, for the desire of the end will point out the means. Desire creates the power. Wherever the mind goes, the energy flows.

You are not a failure if you don't win; you are a failure if you don't participate. It's better to fail with honor than to succeed by fraud.

Purchase gas from the neighborhood gas station even if it costs more. Next winter when it's freezing and your car won't start, you'll be glad they know you andwant to help.

Buy whatever kids are selling on card tables in their front yards.

Buy vegetables from farmers on the side of the highway.

Let people pull in front of you when you're stopped in traffic. And be prepared: those you let in flip you a 'peace sign,' but those you hold up flip you a 'half-a-peace' sign!

You shouldn't go through life with a catcher's mitt on both hands. You need to be able to throw something back.

Many people will walk in and out of your life, but only true friends will leave footprints in your heart.

Conscience is what hurts so bad when everything else feels so good. To handle yourself, use your head; to handle others, use your heart.

Provocative Clarkisms

If a man betrays you once, it is his fault; if he betrays you twice, it is your fault.

Beautiful young people are accidents of nature, but beautiful old people are works of art.

Silent company is often more healing than words of advice.

Wisdom is the gift of the elderly. When an old woman dies an entire library burns to the ground.

Only when the student is ready to learn will the teacher appear.

If someone says something unkind about me, I must live so that no one will believe it. We shouldn't let someone else's words or actions change who we are and what we say and do.

You can tell a lot about a man by the way he handles these three things: a rainy day, lost luggage, and tangled Christmas tree lights.

Even when I have pains, I don't have to be one.

If you pursue happiness, it will elude you. But if you focus on your family, the needs of others, your work, meeting new people, and doing the very best you can, happiness will find you.

Remember to hold hands and cherish the moment, for someday that person will not be there.

We resent in others what we don't like about ourselves. We must be the change we seek in our relationships, at home and at work.

When we stop growing, we put others down out of insecurity to make ourselves feel better about who we are. Remember, green things keep growing, but ripe things go rotten.

The best gift you can give a loved one is your time.

If the grass looks greener on the other side, it's time to fertilize!

People who use themselves up are the happiest.

You can make a living with knowledge, but you can make a life with wisdom.

Good manners will take you where money cannot. Those who help others feel good about themselves are always in demand.

Do the right thing simply because it is the right thing to do.

Do not let what you cannot do interfere with what you can do.

You've got to be before you can do. You've got to do before you can have. You've got to have before you can give. You've got to give before you can take.

To endure is greater than to dare - To tire out hostile fortune - To be daunted by no difficulty - To keep heart when all have lost it - Who can say this is not greatness?

Ten Little Things that Make the Biggest Difference:
- Count your blessings and write "thank you" notespromptly.
- Record your parents' laughter.
- Respect your mom and talk to her often.
- Be someone's hero, inspiration and role model.
- Remember people's names, and respect everyone who works for a living, regardless of their jobs.

- Don't ever be called out on strikes. Go down swinging, and swing for the fence!
- If you cut your own firewood, it warms you twice. Never cut what can be untied.
- Return borrowed vehicles with a full tank of gas.

Don't burn bridges; you'll be surprised how many times you have to cross the river.

When someone hugs you, be the last one to let go.

Seven Things that Require No Talent:
Timeliness, Work Ethic, Effort, Attitude, Passion, Being Coachable, Doing Extra

Seven Things Money Can't Buy:
Time, Love, Happiness, Courage, Intellect, Purpose, A Legacy

The Seven Best Doctors in the World:
Sunshine, Water, Rest, Air, Exercise, Diet, Human Touch

Spiritual Reminders

"Religion is for those who are afraid to go to hell. Spirituality is for those of us who have already been there."

"I am not an atheist. Although the concept of a Master organizer and Supreme Being is complex and vast for our minds to comprehend, we must embrace the mindset of a young child who walks into a large library and says, 'Surely someone must have written all these books."
- Albert Einstein

"Time does not exist – we invented it. Time is what the clock says. The distinction between the past, present and future is only a stubbornly persistent illusion."

"The intellect has little to do on the road to discovery. There comes a leap in consciousness, call it intuition or what you will, the solution comes to you, and you don't know how or why."

"We are souls dressed up in sacred biochemical garments and our bodies are the instruments through which our souls play their music."

"When you examine the lives of the most influential people who have ever walked among us, you discover one thread that winds through them all. They have been aligned first with their spiritual nature and only then with their physical selves."

"One thing I have learned in a long life: that all our science, measured against reality, is primitive and childlike. We still do not know one thousandth of one percent of what nature has revealed to us. It is entirely possible that behind the perception of our senses, worlds are hidden of which we are unaware."

"Everything is determined, every beginning and ending, by forces over which we have no control. It is determined for the insect, as well as for the star. Human beings, vegetables, or cosmic dust, we all danceto a mysterious tune, intoned in the distance by an invisible piper."

"Energy cannot be created or destroyed - it can only be changed from one form to another."

"Everything is energy and that is all there is to it. Match the frequency of the reality you want and you cannot help but get that reality. It can be no other way. This is not philosophy. This is physics."

"We are more than mere mortal beings living on a small planet for a short season. 'For behold, this life is the time for men to prepare to meet God; yea, behold the day of this life is the day for men to perform their labors." - Dieter F. Uchtdorf

"Science and religion are not antagonists. On the contrary, they are sisters. While science tries to learn more about the creation, religion tries to better understand the Creator. While through science man tries to harness the forces of nature around him, through religionhe tries to harness the force of nature within him." - Wernher von Braun (Chief NASA Scientist)

"Can a physicist visualize an electron? The electron is materially inconceivable and yet, it is so perfectly known through its effects that we use it to illuminate our cities, guide our airlines through the night skies and take the most accurate measurements. What strange rationale makes some physicists accept the inconceivable electrons as real while refusing to accept the reality of a Designer on the ground that they cannot conceive Him?"

"In this age of space flight, when we use the modern tools of science to advance into new regions of human activity, our knowledge and use of the laws of nature that enable us to fly to the Moon also enableus to destroy our home planet with the atom bomb. Science itself does not address the question whether we should use the power at our disposal for good or for evil. The guidelines of what we ought to do are furnished in the moral law of God."

Blaise Pascal, Mathematician, Philosopher concluded: There are four outcomes in discussing the existence of God:

If you <u>Do Believe In God</u> and have faith that He influences your mortal journey with His Commandments and determines your eternal destiny – and <u>God Does Exist</u> – This Is Good and you will be blessed and eternally rewarded.

If you <u>Do Believe In God and God Does Not Exist</u> – you are still better off having livedby a higher moral code as an honest, noble, loving, servant leader! This Is Good!

If you <u>Don't Believe In God and God Does Exist</u> – This Is Bad for you in the final judgment and eternal reward, for surely God requires that we do certain things while on earth, and if we don't, we fall short of the glory of God. Eternity is the wrong thing to be wrong about!!

If you <u>Don't Believe In God and God Does Not Exist</u> – You are off the hook, life was just a party with no purpose because we die and cease to exist. Conclusion: If you live your life according to God's Love and Laws regardless if He exists or not – This Is Really Good!

Legacy Lessons

"The paradox of our time in history is that we have taller buildings but shorter tempers, wider freeways but narrower viewpoints. We spend more but have less. We buy more but enjoy less. We have bigger houses and smaller families, more conveniences but less time. We have more degrees but less sense, more knowledge but less judgment. We've learned how to make a living but not a life. We've added years to life not life to years. We've been all the way to the moon and back but have trouble crossing the street to meet a new neighbor. We conquered outer space but not inner space. We've done larger things but not better things." - George Carlin

"A great many people think they are thinking when they are merely rearranging their prejudices. Prejudice is an adverse opinion formed beforehandor without knowledge or examination of the facts. To think means you focus on an examination of the facts and come to an informed decision based on them. Without the whole truth, everything becomes conjecture, theoretical and hypothesis." - WilliamJames

"The man who votes the same ticket in politics, year after year, without caring for issues or fellow men, merely voting in a certain way because he always has voted so, is sacrificing loyalty to truth, to a weak, mistaken, stubborn attachment to a worn-out precedent. Such a man should stay in his cradle all hislife; because he spent his early years there." - William George Jordan

"When we treat a man as he is, we make him worse than he is; but when we treat him as if he is already what he potentially could be, he becomes what he should be." - Goethe

In a Commencement Speech, 2014 actor Jim Carrey said: "You could spend your whole life worrying about the future, but all there will ever be is what's happening here and the decisions we make in this moment, which are based in either love or fear. So many of us choose our path out of fear disguised as practicality. What we really want seems impossibly out of reach - ridiculous to expect. So we never dare to ask the universe for it.

My father could have been a great comedian but he didn't believe that was possible for him. So he made a conservative choice. Instead, he got a safe job as an accountant. When I was 12 years old, he was let go from that safe job and our family had to do whatever we could to survive. That's when I learned you could fail at what you don't want, so you might as welltake a chance at doing what you love."

In an Acceptance Speech at the 2013 Teen Choice Awards Actor Ashton Kutcher said:

"I believe life is mostly about three things:
First. I believe that opportunity looks a lot like hard work. When I was 13 I had my first job carrying shingles up to the roof, and then I got a job washing dishes at a restaurant, and then I got a job in a grocery store deli, and then I got a job in a factory sweeping Cheerio dust off the ground.

And I've never had a job in my life that I was better than. I was always just lucky to have a job, and every job I had was a stepping stone to my next job. And I never quit my job until I had my next job. So opportunities look a lot like work.

Second. Being sexy. The sexiest thing in the entire world, is being really smart - being thoughtful — and being generous. Everything else is crap, I promise you.

Third: When you grow up you tend to get told that the world is the way that it is, and that your purpose isto live your life inside the world and try not to get in too much trouble — maybe get an education and get a job and make some money and have a family.

But life can be a lot broader when you realize one thing: everything around us is made up by people who are no smarter than you. So build your own life that other people can live in. Build a life - don't live one."

"Promise yourself today to be so strong, That nothing can disturb your peace of mind; To look on the bright side of everything and make your dreams come true; To think the best, to forget the mistakes of the past, And to press on to better things; To give so much time to improving yourself that you don't have time to criticize others; To be too large for worries, too noble for anger, too large for fear, And too happy to permit the presence of trouble; To think well of yourself and to proclaim this force to the world. Not in loud words but in great works." - James Talmage

"When I die I don't want to drive up to the pearly gates in a shiny sports car, wearing beautifully tailored clothes, with long, perfectly manicured fingernails and my hair expertly coifed. I want to drive up in an old station wagon that has mud on the wheels from taking kids to Boy Scout camp; to be there with a smudge of peanut butter on my shirt from making sandwiches for a sick neighbor's children; to be there with a little dirt under my fingernails from helpingto weed someone's garden; to be there with children's sticky kisses on my cheeks and the tears of a friend on my shoulder. I want the creator to know I was really here and that I really lived." - Marjorie Hinckley

"I'm not the sort to back away from a fight. I don't believe in shrinking from anything. It's not my speed. I'm a guy who meets adversities head on.

All the screen cowboys behaved like real gentlemen. We didn't drink, we didn't smoke, and why in all my pictures I have never shot a guy in the back.

I guess this is why I only made movies where my character could say what I believed, like: 'A man's got to dowhat a man's got to do. There are some things a man just can't run away from;' 'I won't be wronged, I won'tbe insulted, and I won't be laid a hand on. I don't do these things to other people, and I require the same from them;' and 'All battles are fought by frightened men who'd rather be some place else. Courage is being scared to death and saddling up anyway.'

Bottom line. I believe that a man should talk low, talk slow, don't say too much, and let his actions speak louder than his words, and why I would like to be remembered with the Mexican phrase, 'Feo fuerte y formal,' which means 'he was ugly, strong and had dignity.'" - Actor John 'The Duke' Wayne

"Let every nation know, whether it wishes us well or ill, that we shall pay any price, bear any burden, meet any hardship, support any friend, oppose any foe to assure the survival and the success of liberty. Let us think of education as the means of developing our greatest abilities, because in each of us there is a private hope and dream which, fulfilled, can be translated into benefit for everyone and greater strength for our nation cost of freedom is always high, but Americans have always paid it. Therefore, my fellow Americans, ask not what your country can do for you, ask what you can do for your country."- President John F. Kennedy

Lyrical Poetry

Mathematical Love
(Copyright Dan Clark 1982)

He's teaching her arithmetiche
said it was his mission
He kissed her once, he kissed her twice,
and said, "Now that's addition"

And as he added smack by smack
in silent satisfaction
She sweetly gave the kisses back
and said, "Now that's subtraction"

Then he kissed her, she kissed him,
without an explanation
Then both together smiled and said,
"That's multiplication"

Then dad appeared upon the scene
and made a quick decision
He kicked that kid three blocks away
and said,"That's long division!"

Writing "Unstoppable"

One of the true heroes in my life is the collegiate wrestling champion Anthony Robles. In 2011, Anthony won the National NCAA Wrestling Champion-ship - with only one leg! I was privileged to be asked towrite his acceptance speech as he proudly received the Jimmy Valvano ESPY Award for Courage on nationaltelevision July 14, 2011. With the world watching, Robles humbly spoke:

"At the beginning of my wrestling career, I lost most of my matches, and people said, 'It's okay. I'm proud of you for trying.' This ticked me off so bad! Losing is not okay! What they were really saying was that I was a handicapped kid and should be grateful that I could even participate.

"My dear mother had me when she was sixteen years old. It was the summer before her senior year in high school. My birth dad immediately bailed. I was born with one leg, and my mom could have walked away and given me up for adoption.

"She didn't. While kids at school made fun of me, she taught me to never let what I cannot do interfere with what I can do. "She could have protected me from pain and failure, but she knew it would develop my character and make me strong. So she even let me play football.

And even when my mom got sick at the beginning of my sophomore year in college, and my stepdad walked out on our family and we lost our home, and I wanted to quit wrestling to get a job and help pay the bills, still my mom refused to let any of us give up!"

Robles ended with this poem that I wrote that conveys his understanding of winning:

Unstoppable
(Copyright Dan Clark 2011)

Every soul who comes to earth
With a leg or two at birth
Must wrestle his opponents knowing
It's not what is, it's what can be
that measures worth

Make it hard - just make it possible
And through pain I'll not complain
My spirit is unconquerable
Fearless I will face each foe
For I know I am capable

Making winning personal
I don't care what's probable
Through blood, sweat and tears
I am Unstoppable!

Writing "U2 Eternity"

On October 22 and 23, I had a pinnacle adventure in a 'High Flight' aboard a U2 reconnaissance spy plane. After a flight surgeon gave me a comprehensive examination at the base clinic, the fitting and donning of my 130-pound space suit was complete, and I had finished a half day of ejection seat and cardio training - and physiological and pressurization tests in the altitude chamber - I was ready for my flight.

The next morning at 6:00 am we repeated most of the ordeal, boarded the aircraft with my pilot Gino, and, in a high-performance takeoff where the thick clouds miraculously opened in the nick of time to create a small window of blue sky through which we could climb toward heaven, we accelerated straight up to soar on the edge of the universe.

Although the mission was classified, I can tell you that at 70,000 feet above the surface of the earth you can see two-thirds of the state of California. At 80,000 feet you can see mapped outlines of America. And at 90,000 feet you tear up and feel like you can reach out and touch the face God.

For five hours I sat in the sounds of silence looking at the curvature of the earth, gazing into the breathtaking endless blackness of space, pondering eternity and my place in it.

Part of the Significant Emotional Experience for me was realizing that for those few hours, Gino and I were higher than any other human beings on planet Earth, except for the few astronauts and cosmonauts living in the space station.

It hit me hard that when we die we don't lose our memories of what happened for us, not to us, which means the only things we can take with us when we die are what I had with me in the aircraft:

Education - whatever degree of intelligence and knowledge we attain in this life will rise with usin the next and give us an advantage in the world to come.

Character - how we handle our adversity, which introduces us to our real selves.

Convictions - our deepest beliefs and covenants to give our time, talents, and resources to a cause larger than ourselves.

Legacy - that what we leave behind is what I left on the ground: my reputation and a legacy that included taking the time to make a difference in the lives of my family, friends, and fellow citizens.

Because of this 'S.E.E.' Significant Emotional Event I now realize that what we do for ourselves dies with us. But what we do for others and the world remains and is immortal. I now know that having success is no longer a substitute for being significant. I now know that it's time to minimize our hope for success and maximize the effort required to become significant by focusing not on what's impressive but on what's important.

This 'High Flight' inspired the following poem that captures the essence of this life changing experience, illuminated in a fifteen-minute documentary on YouTube danclarku2spyplane.

U2 Eternity
(Copyright Dan Clark 2010)

Today I woke
Prepared myself both physically and mentally
And breathed only the purest thoughts
to free myself from every negativity

Then suited up and walked to boarda secret
craft to soar beyond the bonds of life's
ordinary gravity

Up, straight up, I shot,
And danced with clouds
until I climbed above them in
high flight to see as far as I could see

I saw the curvature of Mother Earth,
And on the edge of space, if we're alone
A waste of space it is for all humanity

And in the blackness of our universe,
Suspended on the wind above where eagles fly
With grace I hovered, sensing that the best is yet to be

Wherein the sounds of silence realized what
we take with us in death is what I had with me:

Education, character, convictions,
and 'I made a difference' legacy.

Then, with tear-filled eyes, surreal in a tranquil blue-
turning-to-black serenity

My heart stood still in breathtaking humility
As I, in awe, felt His almighty presence
While I gazed into eternity

Dan's Original Songs

Always a Reason to Live
(Copyright Dan Clark 1987)
(Ode to Suicide Prevention)

I've been in stormy weather
I've cried because of fears
But the soul would have no
rainbows
If the eyes possessed no tears

There's always smoke with fire
And usually joy with pain
To appreciate the sunshine
You've gotta have some rain

So if you're down and troubled
No matter what you do
Don't focus on the thistle
The rose will see you through

When your life is broken
It's yourself that you need to forgive
There is light at the end of the tunnel
There is always a reason to live

I've had my share of sadness
I've cried my share of tears
I've fought my way through friendships
But the real ones they last for years

I've stumbled and I've failed some
Been up yea I've been down
But I learned to soar with eagles
Though my feet are on the ground

So if you're down and troubled
No matter what you do
Don't focus on the thistle
The rose will see you through

When your life is broken
It's yourself that you need to forgive
There is light at the end of the tunnel
There is always a reason to live

Don't be afraid of dying
Be afraid you haven't lived
Always rise each time you fall
When your back's against the wall
Eliminate your shame

Your dreams you can reclaim

So if you're down and troubled
No matter what you do
Don't focus on the thistle
The rose will see you through

When your life is broken
It's yourself that you need to forgive
There is light at the end of the tunnel
There is always a reason to live

Pebble In The Shoe

The Grand Teton had
turned me on each year
Prepared to climb her fourteen
thousand feet of fear

I started out determined
To make my dream come true
And no it's not the boulder rocks
That made me stop and get the blues

It was the pebble in the shoe
Yeah the pebble in the shoe
A tiny thing that rubs us raw
'til it cuts through

A mighty clock will stop
'cause of one little screw
A rock chip in the windshield
Will soon crack through

Yeah David killed Goliath
With a slingshot, true
With a stone, no bigger
Than a pebble in the shoe

Some sell their 'Cedes
Cause one cheap part breaks down
Some sell their piano
Cause one key's flat in sound

Some throw the baby out
with the dirty water, true
And no it's not that all is wrong
That causes fools to get blue

It was the pebble in the shoe
Yeah the pebble in the shoe
A tiny thing that rubs us raw
'til it cuts through

A mighty clock will stop
'cause of one little screw
A rock chip in the windshield
Will soon crack through

Yeah David killed Goliath
With a slingshot, true
With a stone, no bigger
Than a pebble in the shoe

They say don't sweat the small stuff
But the small stuff is the clue
You gotta fix the little things
before they fix you

Most start their love with vows
And promise they'll stay true
And no it's not the stumbling blocks
That broke true love in two

It was the pebble in the shoe
Yeah the pebble in the shoe
A tiny thing that rubs us raw
'til it cuts through

Dan Clark

A mighty clock will stop
'cause of one little screw
A rock chip in the windshield
Will soon crack through

Yeah David killed Goliath
With a slingshot, true
With a stone, no bigger
Than a pebble in the shoe

Real Man

I need a man
Who knows happily ever after
is a day-at-a-time proposition
A man who knows making love is
not a three-minute composition

It's a slow dance, full of romance
A walk on the beach in the sand
It's having a whole conversation
just by holding my hand

He will stir deep desirethat
sets me on fire,
to be with him all that I can
No, I won't settle for anything less
than a Real Man

A Real Man's strong in stature,
firm in faith, and kisses slow
He sometimes cries, and when we hug
he's the last one to let go

He worships the ground I walk on
He's my biggest fan
There's nothing like being loved
by a Real Man

I need a man who knows honoring
me is a macho disposition
A man who knows I love you is a
more than words rendition

It's roses for no reason
secret love notes in my drawer
It's making me his equal though he
always gets my door

He will never raise his hand to me
believe in who I am
Yea I can be more than I thought
I could be with a Real Man

He talks to me through touch
I'm swept away in every clutch
We're lovers, but we're best friends too
I like me best when I'm with you

A Real Man's strong in stature,
firm in faith, and kisses slow
He sometimes cries, and when we
hug he's the last one to let go

He worships the ground I walk on
He's my biggest fan
There's nothing like being loved
by this Real Man

Special Man

A little boy wants to be like his dad
So he watches us night and day
He mimics our moves and weighs our words
He steps in our steps all the way

He's sculpting a life we're the models for
He'll follow us happy or sad
And his future depends on example set
'cause the little boy wants to be
just like his dad

A special man talks by example
Takes the time to play and hug his lad
A special man walks by example
The very best friend a growing boy ever had
Any male can be a father
But it takes a special man to be a dad

He needs a hero to emulate
He breathes 'I believe in you'
Would we have him see everything we see
And have him do what we do

When we see the reverence
that sparkles and shines
In the worshipping eyes of our lad
Will we be at peace if his dreams come true
And he grows up to be just like his dad

A special man talks by example
Takes the time to play and hug his lad
A special man walks by example
The very best friend a growing boy ever had
Any male can be a father
But it takes a special man to be a dad

Don't Let This Chance Go By

(Copyright Dan Clark 2000)

Have you ever had the feeling
That time was in your hands
Then you put time off
Until another day

Life can't live without you
Take your dream and make it real
Before the magic of the moment
slips away

Don't let this chance go by
Dig down deep inside you
Find the faith you can't deny
You'll never know if you don't try
Don't let this chance go by

If you look beyond the questions
No mountain can't be moved
You can live your life in a place
you've never been

Every new day is a doorway
So open just as wide
Cause you know you'll never
pass this way again

Don't let this chance go by
Dig down deep inside you
Find the faith you can't deny
You'll never know if you don't try

Cause the same sun that sets
Low Rises so high
Just like tears the rain must fall
If the rainbow's gonna fly

Don't let this chance go by
Dig down deep inside you
Find the faith you can't deny
You'll never know if you don't try
Don't let this chance
Never let the chance go by

You Need a Woman Not a Song
(Copyright Dan Clark 2000)

One night I phoned the Deejay
to request of her a song
A little rhythm for my blues
and some sultry soul to turn me on

Stir me with some classical and a
mix of jazzy smooth
I need a little country cryin' slide
to mellow out my mood

It needs to rock me everyday
and roll me all night long
She said boy, you need a woman,
not a song

You need a woman, not a song
Who with a touch says you belong
Who doesn't love cause you're all that
She loves you cause she's strong

Always there when you're weak
And with harmony sweetens what
now's goin on
Oh yea, you need a woman, not a song

I hung the phone up thinking
bout a woman's melody
Composed by God in the key of peace
like a beautiful symphony

Could just her simple kiss turn my music on
Would making love have tempo changes
sometimes slow, sometimes strong
Yeah, she's the medley, I've
tuned out too long
I need a woman, not a song

A woman doesn't dress up to
be eye-candy for men
It's a competition just
between the women

And no she doesn't love you
cause you're beautiful
You are beautiful because she loves
Tune into her goodness, cause no one
loves you like she does…

You need a woman, not a song
Who with a touch says you belong
Who doesn't love cause you're all that
She loves you cause she's strong

Always there when you're weak
She forgives when you're wrong
And with harmony sweetens
what now's goin on
Oh yea, you need a woman, not a song

In Two More Days Tomorrow's Yesterday

(Copyright Dan Clark 2000)

I used to live my life on time delay
A day behind, a day ahead but
never right away

Hurry up and wait
was a road rage waste of time
Fast, slow, stop, going out of my mind

Tomorrow is the day
I thought would never come
Yesterday and 'used to be's' are
when I got me some

The older I get the better I was
memories change
The only constant's what we rearrange

Past, present, future really are the same
Different order, separate times
all the same game

What will be makes history
this too shall pass away
In two more days, tomorrow's yesterday
Past, present, future all turn to day
In two more days, tomorrow's yesterday

Today is the someday
I longed for yesterday
'I'll wait until tomorrow'
was the cheapest price to pay

The other side seemed greener
talked of glory days of play
Was caught between tomorrow
and yesterday

They say timing's everything
what should be will be
Things happen for a reason
a lifetime guarantee

What goes around comes back
around just by a different name
The more things change
the more they stay the same

Past, present, future
really are the same
Different order, separate times
all the same game

What will be makes history,
this too shall pass away
In two more days, tomorrow's yesterday

Past, present, future all turn today
In two more days, tomorrow's yesterday.

So Have I

(Copyright Dan Clark 2000)

Have you ever been alone
in a crowded room that's full of lies
Have you ever been betrayed
and don't know why

Have you ever felt the backbite
of a friend they then deny
You are not alone, so have I
You are not alone, so have I

Have you ever been lonely
in a lover's arms and cry
Have you ever hurt from a
brutal bad goodbye

Have you ever sobbed so long
you drained your feelings drip-dry
You are not alone, so have I
You are not alone, so have I

Yea I've felt your pain, it's rained,
it's poured on my parade
Yea I've suffered through the blues
of knowing I've been played

So when you hear this too shall pass away
tomorrow's just a day away
And you hang on for one more day and say
I'll try… So have I

Have you ever been afraid that
no one needs you in their life
Have you ever thought
that love has passed you by

Have you ever stopped believing
in yourself and died inside
You are not alone so have I
You are not alone so have I

I have faced my fears and demons
I have beat the odds
I have realized I can only
count on me and God

I have been a broken-winged
bird but now I fly
I pray, you'll say, so have I

Yea I've felt your pain, it's rained
it's poured on my parade
Yea I've suffered through the blues
of knowing I've been played

So when you hear this too shall
pass away, tomorrow's just a day away
And you hang on for one more day and say
I'll try… So have I

Quiet Heroes

The world is full of quiet heroes
who never seek the praise
They're always back off in the shadows
They let us have the limelight days

For this you're the one that I look up to
Because of you I'm free
You set an example I could follow
You helped me see my destiny

So even though my thanks don't show
Unnoticed you will never go
I need to say I love you so
You're my hero.

I've had my share of broken dreams
But you said I could win
You gave me the chance I always needed
To start my dreams again

You took the time to teach and tutor
and show me rules to rise
You changed my fears to glory tears
You're an angel in disguise

I wouldn't be where I am today
I've won my share of times
Unless you coached me through the maze
And pushed me on the hardest climbs

Dan Clark

It's just your style, the extra mile
no glory must be tough
You let me have the accolades
A smile, you said, was just enough

So even though my thanks don't show
Unnoticed you will never go
I need to say I love you so
You're my hero.

All In A Smile

(Ode to Operation Smile)

Have you ever seen a mother cry
I mean because her baby
isn't healthy knows not why

Have you ever heard a mother pray
I mean plead that her new baby will
be whole and well one day

A mother's tears could fill a hundred
cups from her child's pain
And yet she never loses hope
her faith remains

Who will love a motherwho
will help her child Who will
free a spirit who has been
exiled

Listen to the still small voice that
whispers make a choice to serve a
child
And the thanks you get is all in
a smile

Have you ever seen a young child's eyes
The look when they're ashamed of what
you see and seek disguise

Have you ever heard a young child's heart
That beats so loud from fear you'll help
the others then depart

Who will love a mother
who will help her child Who
will free a spirit who has been
exiled

Listen to the still small voice that
whispers make a choice to serve a
child
And the thanks you get
is all in a smile

Faces from so many places
change and smile and glow
A smile will take your heart to
 places words can never go

Who they were before is
just a memory they know
One smile at a time we
can heal the world and so...

Who will love a mother
who will help her child
Who will free a spirit who
has been exiled

Listen to the still small voice
that whispers make a choice
to serve a child
Trust me that the only thanks
you need is in their smile

Only The Elderly Know

Some things are true
whether we believe them or not
Like the old must die, and the
young may no matter how we plot

We won't regret the things we did
 just what we didn't do
Getting old and being oldare
different attitudes

Possessing wealth means nothing
it's the noble use that's great
When much is given, much is now
expected, pass your plate

Life, there's no mistakes,
there's only lessons to be learned
And only those who've lived enough
can teach us and discern

Wisdom is the gift of the elderly
When an old man dies
a library burns to the ground

One old friend is better than
two new ones
Slow and steady wins the race
the elderly have found

The power we desire lives
within us as we go
The important things
the elderly know

Some things are true,
whether we believe them or not
Like you'll make a lousy somebody
else be you, don't be bought

It's not having the best players
it's having the right ones
Not what we do, but who we do it
with is why we won

What keeps us alive and well
is dreaming mighty dreams
Finding meaning, having purpose
matters, so it seems

All we need is to be needed
with good reason to give
And only those who've lived enough
can show us how to live

They say when you lose your dreams
you die so you gotta dream to live
Lifelong learners live long lives
they read and laugh and give

Don't you want to die while climbing
not in the valley low
That's why we honor the elderly
'cause these things they all know

Fly

I'm living on a one way, dead end street
And I don't know how I got there
My house has a circular driveway
Goin' round and round nowhere

The access road's under construction
detour signs since May
On the other side is a boat
without a paddle in the bay

Stuck, down on luck
What on earth's left to try?Fly

When your road gets rough
and your way's not clear
And your wheels fall off and it's
hard to steer
And you hurt so bad you can't
walk, drive or cry…
Fly!

Holding on doesn't make you strong
Sometimes ground control is wrong
When nothing on this earth can alter why
Fly!

I'm working in a store open 24/7with
locks on every door
Sales are slim, it's a tile company
with carpet on their floor

The rat race won't let me stop for gas
And my car's jammed in reverse
So I walk uphill both ways to work
Cause my only other option is a hearse

Stuck, down on luck
What on earth's left to try?
Fly!

When your road gets roughand
your way's not clear
And your wheels fall off and it's
hard to steer
And you hurt so bad you can't walk,
drive or cry…Fly!

Holding on don't make you strong
Sometimes ground control is wrong
When nothing on this earth can alter
why Fly!

You see a bigger picture when
you're high than when you're low
Don't let life's traffic tower
keep you down or tell you no

When your road gets rough
and your way's not clear
And your wheels fall off and it's
hard to steer
When nothing on this earth
can alter why
Fly! Baby Fly! Fly! Fly!

Life Is A Long Country Road

(Copyright Dan Clark 2000)

To get to Grandpa's house you've
gotta take the highway south
Then turn off onto Deer Creek
Road and drive

It's steep and dusty, rocky with a
rut six inches deep When you get
there you'rejust glad that you're
alive

But Grandpa always laughs and
says his road is just like life
Don't get into a rut, it's tough to steer

Just hold on with both hands
and stay on higher ground you'll see
Though out of sight your
destination's clear

No one said that life would be a
smooth path from your door
With perfect weather every day
and a sale at every store

No there's no express lane or a
way around wide loads
Life is a long country road

Dan Clark

Driving back from Grandpa's
for the thousandth time it seemed
I reminisced on all our memories
shared

Fishing, catching nothing
Hunting never seeing deer
It's not the destination it's the
journey he declared

Winding turns with ups and downs
I knew the road by heart
Though rough I took
for granted it's okay

Suddenly I hit a bump
that wasn't there before
Skidding I recovered thinking
what would Grandpa say

Grandpa said if you start your trip
with the end in mind you'll see
No matter what may happen
'long the way there's just one key

It's all about the road you're on
the right road, don't pretend
Not a race or competition, only
driving till the end

No one said that life would be a
smooth path from your door
With perfect weather every day
and a sale at every store

No there's no express lane or a
way around wide loads
Life is a long country road

How Poor The Wealthy Are

A wealthy father took his daughter
to the countryside
To show her how some farmers live
and the money crunch they hide

Yet after two nights father asked her
what she'd learned so far
She answered thanks for showing
me how poor we are

We have one dog they have four
We buy food they grow and store
Our pool goes to the garden bend
Their's is a creek that has no end

We have a small yard they have
fields that go beyond our site
We have lanterns from Brazil
and they have stars at night

Walls protect us, friends protect
them, love is never far
It's amazing how dirt poor
the wealthy are

Now back at the mansion
all their money had no charm
She had servants serving her
but they serve others on the farm

Surrounded by clothes, jewelry
and her choice of fancy cars
Again she said 'dad thanks for
showing me how poor we are'

Have you noticed if money's
the goal more is never enough
And there's never a funeral procession
including a truck full of stuff

True riches are family, friends,
we've got to raise our bar
It's amazing how dirt
poor the wealthy are

We have one dog they have four,
We buy food they grow and store
Our pool goes to the garden bend
Their's is a creek that has no end

We have a small yard, they have
fields that go beyond our site
We have lanterns from Brazil
and they have stars at night

Walls protect us, friends
protect them, love is never far
It's amazing how dirt
poor the wealthy are!

Be Who You Is

A father came home straight
from work and laid more work
sheets out
His little boy didn't understand
what deadlines were about

Dad told him he would need an
hour then they'd swing the bat
But his little guy didn't understand
'An hour, how long's that?'

So Dad took out a magazine
and found a photograph
Then ripped it in a hundred
pieces and ripped them all in half

Dad thought it'd take him half the
night to make the puzzle whole
But his little guy came right back
to show he'd accomplishd his goal

'How'd you get it done so fast?'
he'd foiled Daddy's plan
'On the flip side of the world'
he said 'was a picture of a man

When I got the man right
it was plain to see
When I get the man right
the world is right for me'

Dad smiled and said, 'You're
right to you you must be true
If you keep trying to be like me
then who's gonna be you

You'll make a lousy somebody
else so be who you is
'Cause if you is who you ain't
then you ain't who you is!'

Ten years later, Dad still workin
home with papers out
His teenage son had come to know
what deadlines were about

Graduation, movin on
his eyes were full of tears
He hadn't spent much time
with Dad
his future full of fears

He asked, 'Dear Dad, how
much you make? What for one
full hour?'
Proudly he said, 'Hundred bucks
I climbed the corporate tower'

His son walked out and got his
savings bond he'd saved for school
'I'd like to buy an hour of your
time just by the pool'

Guilty tears began to flow
'I've blown it bad, my son
I've sold out chasing dollars
I tried to be like everyone

I should have been my own
Man it's what I always teach
I should be more like you son
and practice what I preach'

His son smiled and said, 'You're
right to you, you must be true
If you keep trying to be like me
then who's gonna be you

You'll make a lousy somebody
else so be who you is
'Cause if you is who you ain't
then you ain't who you is!'

Father, son began to run
and share themselves at last
They lived a lifetime every day
and made up for the past

And the secret to their closeness
was just being who they is
'Cause if you is who you ain't
then you ain't who you is.

Hard To Hear What You Say

Still water runs deep
A quiet man has a lot of things
cookin'
Silence can speak
You can see a lot just by lookin'

We need to listen between the lines
And notice all the warning signs
To find what's real, we've gotta feel
Cause feeling's what defines

If you really love me, show me
If you need me, really know me
I'd rather see a preacher live
than hear his sermon Sunday

If you really gamble, go me
Cause table talk don't throw me
Actions speak so loud it's hard
to hear what you say

Smooth talkin' is cheap
His 'what's inside' must match
his livin'
Real men will weep
You can gain a lot just by givin'

We need to put intentions aside
And break on through to the doin'
side
To find ourselves we lose ourselves, in
service love abides

Walk beside me don't just point
the way
Holding me, says so much more
than words could ever say...

If you really love me, show me
If you need me, really know me
I'd rather see a preacher live than
hear his sermon Sunday

If you really gamble, go me
Cause table talk don't throw me
Actions speak so loud it's
hard to hear what you say

Keep On Swinging

At a baseball game, the same
guy struck out three times in a row
In fact he hadn't had a hit
since seven games ago

In the final inning, bases loaded,
two outs, he's at bat
The coach called time and walked
out to home plate to have a chat

He said it's not the slump you're
in that defines you today
It's what you plan to become
and facing what's now in your way

If he throws it hard or changes
updon't lose your nerve
Like the road of life a corner's
not the end, it's just a curve

Yea a broken clock is
right twice a day
Never give up, it's the price
that everyone can pay

No matter what your past has been
your future starts today
To get out of a slump, you gotta
keep on swinging till you find a way

The pitcher wound up, threw
high heat he swung and missed again
Then strike two, then a ball thatnearly
hit him in the chin

But he got up, brushed himself off
grabbed his bat and stared him down
Then pointed at the fence to say
the next pitch he would pound

The pitcher wound up one more
time to finish off the game
But he hadn't heard the coach's words
and that the batter thought the same

The pitch, the swing, he hit
a home further than just far
It cleared the stadium and hit
the pitcher's brand new car

Keep on swinging, that's the key
In ten times up to bat
the superstars only hit three
Yea a broken clock is
right twice a day
Never give up, it's the price
that everyone can pay

No matter what your past has been
your future starts today
To get out of a slump, you gotta
keep on swinging till you find a way

Winners Make Others More

Twas a fifty-yard dash
at an Olympic race
Three special people
with courage and grace

Two were in wheelchairs
and one runner stood
At the sound of the gun
all three gave all they could

Jenny went weaving
but would finish the race
Joe's chair hit the wall
stranded in place

Kim ran ahead yet with
ten yards to go
He looked back to check
up on Jenny and Joe

Winners and losers aren't
made with a score
It's not who's the fastest
it's deep to the core

It's never just sometime
but an all-the-time thing
It's how much we give,
and it's how much we bring

Winners and losers aren't
made with a score
Winners make others more

Seeing Joe's chair stuck
Kim stopped and turned
The fans went real quiet
as they saw his concern

Kim ran to help Joe and
pushing his chair
Together they finished
the race as a pair

Jenny had won it and
second was Joe
Because Kim was pushing
he took last you know

Yet the crowd started
cheering and chanting
Kim's name
With tears they now knew
the real goal of life's game

It's that 'something more'
that makes us rare
That 'something more'
that winners share
Aware through 'something
more' we dare to care

Winners and losers
aren't made with a score
It's not who's the fastest
it's deep to the core

It's never just sometime
but an all-the-time thing
It's how much we give
and it's how much we bring

Winners and losers aren't
made with a score
Winners make others more

Last Cliche'
(Copyright Dan Clark 2000)

There are lessons from the heart
we should remember as we roam
Like no success can compensate
for failure in the home

Another teaches broken
clocks are still right twice a day
So don't give up on anyone
God makes no junk they say

You can't increase a man's
performance making him feel bad
Failure's not a person
its events that make you sad

No matter what your past has
Been you have a spotless future
Live and let live, laugh, and love
forgiveness you must nurture

I know you've heard these
catchy quotes at home, at work
and play
And busy complicating life
so blow off what they say

But when the lessons learned are
lost and you can't find your way
There's always hope for holding on
Til you're down to your last cliché

We don't care about storms
but did you bring in the ship
If you're burned out it's okay
cause at one time you were lit

If you're defined by what you
doinstead of who you are
You're just a human doing
not a human being star

Nuggets of pure wisdom
in a rhythm when they're told
Cutting through the clutter
good clichés expose the gold

Sage's lectures for the ages
teaching right from wrong
And the best part is they're
usually one line long

I know you've heard these catchy
quotes at home, at work and play
And busy complicating life,
so blow off what they say

But when the lessons learned
are lost and you can't find your way
There's always hope for holding on
Til you're down to your last cliché

If You Have To Tell Them That You Are Then You Aren't

(Copyright Dan Clark 2000)

A famous actor sat back in the
corner out of sight
A hundred movies and two
Oscars clearly proved his might

The emcee introduced the
latest starlets on TV
Yet never mentioned this true
legend he had failed to see

Suddenly a hostess spied him,
whispered 'You're the star
Don't you feel left out, no one
acknowledged who you are?'

He smiled, if you have to tell them
that you are then you are not
Tooting your own horn is like
the cowboy with a big hat
braggin' 'bout cows he ain't got

Like a weatherman who thinks
he has to tell us when it's hot
If you have to tell them
that you are… you're not

Dan Clark

Two wealthy men each donated
a million to the school
One said that a building would
be named for him, his rule

The ceremony covered on TV
was this man's plan
With not a single mention
of the other donor man

Suddenly a trustee recognized this
humble star
And asked, 'Why are you keeping
Press from knowing who you are?'

The great ones quietly will strengthen,
softly flex their might
The toughest, baddest dudes we know
They never have to fight

Giving, doing when you'llnever
get the credit due
Is the loving form of living, private
victory sees you through

He smiled, if you have to tell them
that you are then you are not
Tooting your own horn is like
the cowboy with a big hat braggin'
'bout cows he ain't got

Like a weatherman who thinks
he has to tell us when it's hot
If you have to tell them
that you are… you're not.

142

How You Spent Your Dash

(Copyrighted song by Dan Clark 2019 - with permission
adapted from the poem by Linda Ellis)

An old man wrinkled in his face
and withered in his hands
Died last week at 96
left footprints in our sands

Thousands came to mourn
and show respect for a life so fine
His tombstone said 1903 dash 1999

The preacher read his date of birth
and the date of death brought tears
But the part we celebrate he said is
the dash between those years

Sure the wealthy man had houses
cars and gobs of cash
But what mattered most was the way
he loved and how he spent his dash

Life might only last a while so slow
down watch and feel
Take the time to understandwhat's
true and all that's real

Treat each other with respect
decide all you could change
Then live your life with the time
that's left while you still can rearrange

So when your eulogy is readand
your actions they rehash
You'll be proud of the things
they say bout how you spent your dash

The old man's life was a testament
of service above self
He gave more than he took
selfishness put upon a shelf

The preacher said he never angered
and was very slow to speak
He listened in between the lines
compassion he would seek

He loved to live and lived to love
and more often wore a smile
The preacher said he even thought
the homeless had great style

So he said the dash means all
the time you spent alive on earth
And all of you who love this
man know what this line is worth

Sleep On A Windy Night

(Copyright Dan Clark 2000)

A young man came a calling
was answering the ad
The farmer needed hired help
promised all he had

The farmer asked, 'Why hire you?'
He said, 'I'll do what's right
You'll never have to worry
I can sleep on a windy night'

Late that evening clouds rolled
in disaster dead ahead
The farmer called the lad for help
but was sound asleep in bed

He raced out but the gates were
tied the yard was fastened tight
Everything was safe, he smiled,
"I can sleep on a windy night"

You can sleep through the night
if inside your skies are blue
Takin' care of business
before it takes care of you

No matter what the forecast
if prepared there is no plight
While others stay awake and stir
you can sleep on a windy night

A traveling man was lonelywent
out to get a drink
She caught his eye and flashed
some thigh, his flesh began to think

A storm was raging, lust was
caging him and squeezing tight
But he didn't stay, with his wife away
he'd rather sleep on a windy night

Back at home with kids tucked in
the weather turned real bad
The frightened children climbed
in bed and snuggled up to dad

'Will the house blow down
will the windows break
or did the builder build it right?'

Everything's secure, we're safe
and sound til morning light
He said, 'I am the carpenter
you can sleep on this windy night'

No matter what the forecast
if prepared there is no plight
While others stay awake and stir
you can sleep on a windy night.

Fail My Way To Success

On top of old smoky
all covered with snow
I lost my best bird dog
by aiming too low

So I raise my sights
and fire at bliss
reloading and never quit
Cause it's better to shoot
for the stars and miss
than to aim for manure and hit

When there is no vision
the people parish too
blind to ever progress
So I guess I better
keep keeping on til I
fail my way to success

We're The Change We Seek

(Copyright Dan Clark 2009)
(Theme Song written for the Festival of Thinkers in Abu Dhabi UAE)

When the winds of change start to blow
Some build shelters, others go
and take their hearts to places
where their minds alone can't know

Seduced by the land of the seven sands
where falcons soar, and camels stand
as witnesses to what has been
inspiring we can

Like the million stars in Arabian nights
alone we shine, together we're light

We're hearts, we're hope, we're minds
pondering what to do
We're peace, we're love, a festival of
thought, a quest for the truth

We are, we were, we have, we will
still pushing toward each distant hill
We're the change we seek
til destiny's fulfilled

When a troubled world starts to cry
Some blame others some ask why
and leave their footprints in our sand
as wisdom from on high

Standing on the shoulders of those before
on their wind our wings will soar
beyond the boundaries of our minds
to heaven's door

Like the million stars in Arabian nights
alone we shine, together we're light

We're hearts, we're hope, we're minds
pondering what to do
We're peace, we're love, a festival of
thought, a quest for the truth

We are, we were, we have, we will
still pushing toward each distant hill
We're the change we seek
til destiny's fulfilled.

Will I See You Again?

(Copyright Dan Clark 1984)(Sung at Dad's funeral)

There's a feeling stuck inside me
'bout a leader of life's band
You're the one who showed me how
to play, and whispered 'Yes, you can!'

You taught me life and living loveyour
wisdom was my friend
Will I see you again?

There's a memory-making motion
'bout a beacon burning bright
You're the one who turned my
troubled times from darkness into light

Your guiding ray unveiled the way
you counseled 'til the end
Will I see you again?

You always cautioned at the door
'Remember who you are'
'Cause I guess you saw in
me what I could be

I needed you to need me, and
you stretched a helping hand
Unselfishly, so tenderly
left footprints in my sand
You let me understand

Dan Clark

There's a notion nestled in me
'bout the rules of the Master Man
Even though you lost the battle here
you won the war, His plan

I'll miss your hugs and eyes that grin
but we'll meet once more so long 'til then
When I see you again
Yes, I'm gonna see you again.

May You Never Fly Alone

(Copyright Dan Clark 2012)
(Ode to the pilots in the U.S. Air Force)

May you always have
a cloudless sky ahead
May the wind beneath your wings
be prayers we've said

May your HUD show coast is clear
with tanks full free to roam
May you always have a tailwind
that will hurry you back home

May you always know we love
you and support you carry on
May you know you've got some
wingmen on the ground while
you are gone

Flying Mach 2, hair on fire,
9 g's crunchin breath
Fly, fight, win, Libertas Vel Mors
it's 'liberty or death'

Falcons, Eagles, Buffs and Hogs
show air supremacy
Joints and Raptors stealthy flex
don't mess with the brave and free

When duty, honor, country call
you deep in the danger zone
May God bless and protect you
May you never fly alone.

May you always feel the
sunshine's warm embrace
May you soar above the rest
with an angel's grace

May you know we think about
the sacrifice you daily make
May you see we're proud of you
for what you do for freedom's sake

May you always know your service
matters now and years beyond
May you know we'll guard the Fort
your family's safe while you are gone

Flying Mach 2, hair on fire
9 g's crunchin breath
Fly, fight, win, Libertas Vel Mors
its 'liberty or death'

Falcons, Eagles, Buffs and Hogs
show air supremacy
Joints and Raptors stealthy flex
don't mess with the brave and free

Gunfighters, Warbirds, 8th, 23rd
9th, 3rd, 12th, Creech Thunderbirds
Fearless warriors, heroes of the sky
Here's to you, your legacy will never die

When duty, honor, country call
you deep in the danger zone
May God bless and protect you
May you never fly alone

Pledge to the Red, White, and Those in Blue

(Copyright Dan Clark 1991)
(Ode to Fire Fighters, Police Officers, FirstResponders)

It's early morn the sun
is shining worry not around
Parents, sons and daughters
Working birds outside the only
sound

Suddenly a tragedy, a crash, a fire lit
Everyone was stunned and
ran outside to see who done it

While everyone was running
from the burning building there
The fire fighters ran right in,
right past them not a care

And officers raced round to
Help some folks they never knew
Yes let us honor heroes
God bless all those in blue

They're roses sent from heaven
dedicated to our cause
Saving lives and selflessly stay
strong without applause

Every race, creed, gender serves
while families wait return
Giving everything they have
sometimes their lives we learn

Yes they're heroes, pray for them
please God bless what they do
Let us honor, let us pledge to the
red, the white and those in blue

Late at night the moon full
brightand quiet is the sound
Then suddenly the peace is
shattered hope is not around

Screams with tears and cries from
Fear oh who will help us through
The only ones who are never done
the 'Bravehearts' dressed in blue

Real-life heroes every day
we take their jobs for granted
Til crisis hits and we wake up our
 views no longer slanted

We all love you, we all need you
thanks for all you do
When we stand to pledge or
kneel to pray we always think
of you

They're roses sent from
heaven dedicated to our cause
Saving lives and selflessly
staystrong without applause

Every color, race and creed,
serve while families wait return
Giving everything they have,
sometimes their lives we learn

Yes they're heroes, pray for them
please God bless what they do
Let us honor, let us pledge to the
red, the white and those in blue.

Growing Old Together

(Copyright Dan Clark 1991)

Today I saw a couple holding
withered hands to talk
I saw them snuggle in real close
to finish their long walk

I saw him open up her door
and walk around the car
She leaned across to open his
and kissed her long-time star

Later on I saw them by the
pool beside the gym
Though there were younger, fitter
men she still had eyes for him

So I asked what their sweet secret
was for lasting living love
He smiled, 'It's just one thing my
friend, the only thing I think of

'We're growing old together' the
old man said 'can't you see'
Then he looked at her so differently
than the way he looked at me

I wake up to the thought of our
long-term plan that's still clear

When others walk away we
stay forever means from here

Growing old together
day-by-day its destiny
We're growing old together
and the best is yet to be

I looked inside myself and saw
a heart that had been used
To the point where my emotions
had been toyed with and abused

I saw devotion to the notion
love was just romance
To the point where my desire
burned to take most any chance

And yes in watching this fine pair
who still played truth or dare
Together 50 years still dreaming,
planning things they'd share

I asked him what their secret was
to a love I'd never known
He smiled and said, 'It's just one thing
through thick and thin we've grown'

'We're growing old together,' the old
man said, 'can't you see'
Then he looked at her so differently
than the way he looked at me

I wake up to the thought of our
long-term plan that's still clear
When others walk away we stay
forever means from here

Dogs Never Lie About Love

(Copyright Dan Clark 1991)

I think I'm going out of my mind
Still searching for the perfect love
the one most never find

Venus women, men from Mars
our differences defined
Yet here we are still playing games
the same lame rules the same old grind

Where is real, I yearned to feel
connection blessed above
We should show what canines know
Dogs never lie about love

Dogs never lie about love
Open, unconditional, honest,
never fictional
When I'm home she wants me
like a cold hand needs a glove

Will not judge, won't hold a grudge
when tough times come she stays
won't budge
When I'm gone I'm the only one
she's thinking of…

With a knock or doorbell ring
she guards the door
I'm her most important guy
the one that she adores

The later I am, the more
jumping and barking for me
Doesn't care about past loves
examining with jealousy

She accepts me just the way
I am like God above
Canines no true loyalty
Dogs never lie about love

Dogs forgive, forget the past
know what it takes to make love last
If they could talk they'd tell us
life without true love's a crime
Porsche, Harley happy cause
they're loving all the time

Dogs never lie about love
Open, unconditional honest,
never fictional
When I'm home she wants me
like a cold hand needs a glove

Will not judge, won't hold a grudge
when tough times come she stays
won't budge
When I'm gone I'm the only one she's
thinking of…
Dogs never lie about love!

Christmas Songs

Only Heaven Knows

A child sits silent looking round
a wonder in his eyes
Questioning the world about him
full of pure surprise

Why is water blue, the grass
so green, the sky so high
Why are there so many fish and
how come birds can fly

Why are people black, white,
brown and why's a rose a rose
Really only heaven knows

Older, he's a father now with
questions still unclear
What's the purpose of this life
and why are we all here

Who conceived this human
race short, fat, skinny, tall?
And who made God, and
why be good or be at all?

Which religion is the truth
that surely one God chose
Really only heaven knows

Only heaven knows all answers
where and why life flows
Interpretation of a book
won't change how it all goes

Preachers fight, religions kill,
they speak and violence grows
All in the name of answers that
only heaven knows

Why are there religious wars
'tween Muslim, Christian, Jew
When Abraham taught all his
children bout the God he knew

They argue over prayer and
clothing, women's rights and laws
Music, dancing, scriptural doctrine,
each claims has their flaws

Does this bring rewards forever
and how our judgment goes
Really only heaven knows

What about hope, charity,
forgiveness and love
Is this not pure religion and
for all and from above

Radical fanaticals don't represent
God's will
Serving, doing right, brings
peace on earth and life fulfilled

Only heaven knows all answers
where and why life flows
Interpretation of a book
won't change how it all goes

Preachers fight, religions kill,
they speak and violence grows
All in the name of answers that
only heaven knows

I believe the same God
who made me, also made you
So when we hate and hinder
surely God gets the blues

Thus, let us live our lives in
a selfless way that always shows
We actually live and love because
we know what heaven knows

Christmas State of Mind

The war was on, the fighting
fierce now in its 7th year
But soon they'd ease their anger
as the holiday was near

The generals told their troops
to cease their fire Christmas Day
And so they did, then realized
it was still a day away

Father'd been away on business
gone for two weeks straight
His little family needed him but
working wouldn't wait

He hustled home for Christmas
Eve to share gifts Christmas Day
Then realized through time travel
change was still a day away

Christmas can come more
than once a year
A baby born in Bethlehem
began a message clear

If one day we can honor foes
and love so family knows
Every day can be that kind
It's all about a Christmas state of mind

We sing, 'let there be peace on
earth' and 'give peace a chance'
While politician's play their
games of power, land, romance

Summits here and meetings there
they fight to make peace stay
Yet every time they're interviewed
they're still a day away

What if there were no more days
except the one to day
No other chance to take a stance
no other price to pay

Even if it wasn't Christmas would
you serve and give
Would you be more than you have
been with one more day to live

Christmas can come more
than once a year
A baby born in Bethlehem
began a message clear

Christmas state of mind is not
religion that you find
It's a way of living daily life
that Christ began at Christmas time

Let's make each day a Christmas day
It's all about a Christmas state of mind

The Carpenter's Son

(Copyright Dan Clark 2000)

Joseph knew his newborn son was special
Joseph knew an angel gave his name
Jesus would go on to be redeemer
But how did he learn who and why he came

Joseph must have taught his son of Mary
Joseph must have taught his son to pray
At 12 years old alone he taught in temples
Cause Joseph's words inspired him each day

Christmas celebrates the birth of Jesus
Virgin Mother Mary's honored too
But don't forget the carpenter
who taught his son his trade
30 years of mentoring the things
they must have made

Don't forget example is the
greatest way to teach
That Jesus taught what he had seen
then practiced what he preached

Christmas celebrates his birth
and everything He's done
Yeah, God's his father
but He's the carpenter's son

Joseph must have taught his son to listen
Joseph must have taught his son to love
Jesus knew the law and quoted prophets
Cause Joseph knew it too taught from above

Joseph's message fit with his son's gospel
That's why he qualified to be his guide
He and Heavenly Father loved their Jesus
And they both wept when he was crucified

Christmas celebrates the birth of Jesus
Virgin mother Mary's honored too
But don't forget the carpenter
who taught his son his trade
30 years of mentoring the things
they must have made

Don't forget example is the
greatest way to teach
That Jesus taught what he had seen
then practiced what he preached

Christmas celebrates his birth
and everything He's done
Yeah, God's his father
but He's the carpenter's son.

Joseph didn't know He'd walk on water
Joseph didn't know He'd heal the blind
But as his son grew Joseph knew
his mission was divine
And so he proudly cried at the cross
that He'd saved all mankind

Joseph held the Blessed Mary crying out
'Oh Heavenly Father what are we to do?
Yes you're weeping, but don't forget
that He is our son too!'

Yeah, Christmas celebrates Christ's
birth and everything He's done
We know God's His father,
but He's also the carpenter's son.

They Already Crucified Him
(Copyright Dan Clark 2000)

A father and his kids were
Christmas shopping at the mall
Toy store after store
To find a sold out doll

Everything imaginable his
children yearned to buy
Hours later at the elevator
he would sigh

Overwhelmed to go to every
open house at night
Overweight from tasting every
party treat in sight

Pressured to get perfect gifts
for each one on his list
On the crowed elevator
mad, he shook his fist

Whoever started this whole
Christmas thing should think
again
We should track 'em down
and shoot him on a whim

Suddenly a voice whispered,
'Whoa news is grim
You're too late they already
crucified Him.

A dad with no money was depressed
at Christmas time How he'd pay for
gifts without an extra dime

Then he lost his job Could
Santa still arrive
Lost face with family
Chose death over alive

When he went to end it all
He walked across a park
Passed carolers through the
lights and hid in the dark

Feeling life too painful
His priorities now blurred
Went to pull the trigger
When a miracle occurred

A voice said Christ was born
in a manger cold and dim
Mocked and scorned His trials
were tough
Then they crucified Him

Suddenly he didn't feel
His life was so grim
Yes my life is hard
but they crucified Him

What is Christmas, why Christmas,
surely not for elves
It's 'bout the birth of our sweet
brother, like no other
And what He came to do that
we could not do for ourselves

Crazy Christmas Fun

Jolly Old Saint Nicholas
(Copyright Dan Clark 1991)

Jolly old Saint Nicholassitting
in his thong
Now retired in Miami
snowsuit seems so wrong

Checks his list to see who's
badand disregards the good
Only cares about the girls
gone wild down in the hood

Still has toys, delivers gifts,
but not in his big sled
Reindeer hate humidity,
it's Harley rides instead

There's still Christmas, he just
gave Tim Allen something new
Santa's now a home boy hip hop
happenin with his crew

He still chuckles ho, ho, ho
in South Beach he is right
Women throw themselves at him
it's party time each night

Yo, yo Nick has quite the crib
with a backyard boat and doc
Got tired of the travel, he's now
Nikki from the block

Shaved his beard, got a thick gold
chain and a cool Rudolf tattoo
Says better pout, cry, I'm telling
you why the mistletoe pulls through

He tried out, but was way too
stout to be a 'Chippendale'
So he's now a 'Chips-ahoy' dancer
called 'Jolly Old Beached Whale!

The Night Before Christmas

Twas the night before Christmas
and all through the house
Things were real mellow
even Irving the mouse

The boots were hung up
the incense was lit
In hope that Saint Nick
would soon do his bit

The tree was decked outit
was really a site
With love beads and flowers
and a flashing strobe light

Wearing my T-shirt from
Woodstock NationI was
just getting into some
good meditation

My chick was doingsome
yoga in bed
Munching a fruitcake while
propped on her head

Then pow! In the night
a hullabaloo
It shook the waterbed
and woke up old blue

I stumbled around and
tripped on my beard
It stuck to my toes and
felt really weird

When I got to the window
I was really uptight
Cause the scene I perceived
was a mind-blowing site

What through my shades did
I see through the snow
But eight tiny mooses
in a wild UFO

With a big dude inside
looking kinky and groovy
I flashed is this Nick or
some kind of movie

They came from the
cosmos like a far out caboose
And this fat cat kept yelling
at each midget moose

'Right on dasher, on dancer,
Rudolf be mean
Get your bods in high gear
now and move this machine'

Then onto the roof they
flew with a shout
The whole cosmic crew
really freaked me out

They caused such a hassle
and made such a fuss
I thought the fuzz would
be called down on us

He zapped toward the chimney
leaped in with a dive
Then hit, rolled and stoodup
shook off, still alive

His duds were all fur trimmed
in leather and suchHe came in
stone funky
he was really too much

His backpack was painted
with black lights festoon
Full of albums and posters
and a neon balloon

His eyes a light show, his
beard did glow bright
A plastic fantastic
kaleidoscope site

He looked like a guru
this beautiful cat
I thought this cool dude
surely knows where it's at

'Don't want to sound heavy'
he said with a grin
'My message is simple
so dig it tune in

I brought you some goodies
but that's not the thing
My real trip is bringing
good vibes to this scene

So we wrapped til dawn
about peace, love and truth
Then he said, 'Gotta split or
I'm late to Duluth'

He wiggled his noseand
finished his bit
And straight up the smoke
hole this fat cat did split

He spun from the roof
and into the air
And yelled, 'Get your head
straight you people down there

We're brothers and sisters
forgive - be the light
Be kind and we'll all have
a Merry Christmas tonight!'

Thankful
(A Song Medley Remembers When)

As a writer and author of 37 books, I still am in awe of those creative souls who pen lyrical poetry and put it to music. I am grateful for songwriters and their songs that help us 'remember when,' and teach and tutor us in a deep and soulful way about time, life, peace, country, love, and leaving no regrets.

So in thanksgiving to you and to my colleagues around the world, I am sending you this simple wish, itemized in the followingmedley of some favorite tunes:

Yesterday, all my troubles seemed so far away, Now it looks as though they're here to stay, Oh I believe in yesterday.

So I question: why am I fighting to live, If I'm just living to fight, Why am I trying tosee, When there ain't nothing in sight, Why am I trying to give, When no one gives me a try, Why am I dying to live, If I'm just living to die.

But then, every time: I find myself in times of trouble, Mother Mary comes to me, Speaking words of wisdom, let it be - And when the broken hearted people, Living in the world agree, There will be an answer, let it be - For though they may be parted, There is still a chance that they will see, There will be an answer, let it be.

So I've decided to: Imagine there's no countries, It isn't hard to do, Nothing to kill or die for, And no religion too - Imagine no possessions, I wonder if you can, No need for greed or hunger, A brotherhood of man - Imagine all the people, Living life in peace - You may say I'm a dreamer, But I'm not the only one, I hope someday you'll join us, And the world will live as one.

But until then, let us honor our Airmen, Marines, Sailors, and Soldiers who explain: I don't do it for the money, there's bills thatI can't pay, I don't do it for the glory, I just do it anyway, Providing for our future's my responsibility, Yeah I'm real good under pressure, being all that I can be - I can't call in sick on Mondays when the weekend's been too strong, I just work straight through the holidays, Sometimes all night long.

And I will always do my duty, no matter what the price, I've counted up the cost, I know the sacrifice - No I don't want to die for you, But if dying's asked of me, I'll bear that cross with honor, 'Cause freedom don't come free, When liberty's in jeopardy I will always do what's right, I'm out here on the front lines, Sleep in peace tonight - I'm an American soldier who stands for good and right.

Which reminds us we should never take our freedom for
granted, and to leave no regrets, so: I went skydiving, I
went rocky mountain climbing, I went two point seven
seconds on a bull named Fu Man Chu - And I loved
deeper,And I spoke sweeter, And I gave forgiveness
I'd been denyin,' So someday I hope you get the chance
- To live like you were dyin.'

Which takes me back to: The memory of, Thedance we
shared 'neath the stars above, For a moment all the world
was right, How could I have known that you'd ever say
goodbye – And now I'm glad I didn't know, The way it
all would end, the way it all would go, Our lives are
better left to chance, I could have missed the pain, But
I'd have had to miss the dance.

So I hope you'll always: feel small when you stand beside
the ocean, Whenever one door closes I hope one more
opens, Promise me that you'll give faith a fighting
chance, And when you get the choice to sit it out or
dance, I hope you dance.

And that you'll dance with me because: I thinkabout the
years I spent just passing through, I'd like to have the
time I lost and give it back to you, But you just smile and
take my hand, You've been there and understand it's
part of a grander plan - This much I know is true, That
God blessed the broken road, That led me straight to
you.

Which makes me say: When your legs don't work like they used to before, And I can'tsweep you off of your feet, Will your mouth still remember the taste of my love? Will your eyes still smile from your cheeks? And, darling, I will be loving you 'til we're 70, And, baby, my heart could still fall as hard at 23, And I'm thinking 'bout how people fall inlove in mysterious ways, Maybe just the touchof a hand, Well, me—I fall in love with you every single day, And I just wanna tell you I am.

And now that you're gone I remind you: The wild and windy night that the rain washed away, Has left a pool of tears crying for the day, Why leave me standing here, let me knowthe way - Many times I've been alone and many times I've cried, Anyway you'll never know the many ways I've tried - And still theylead me back to the long and winding road, You left me standing here a long, long time ago - Don't leave me waiting here, lead me to your door.

So I proudly sing: If tomorrow all the things were gone I worked for all my life, And I had to start again, With just my children and my wife, I thank my lucky stars, To be living here today, 'Cause the flag still stands for freedom, And they can't take that away - And I'm proudto be an American, Where at least I know I'm free, And I won't forget the men who died, Who gave that right to me, And I'd gladly stand up next to you, And defend Her still today, 'Cause there ain't no doubt, I love this land - God Bless the U.S.A.

Other Books Available By Dan Clark

The Art of Significance
-Achieving The Level BeyondSuccess
(Audiobook Also Available)

The Art of Significance
Study GuideTraining Manual

The Art of Significant Relationships
– 15 Experts On What, Why and How

The Art of Raising Significant Children

Influential Impact
- The Art ofSignificant
Leadership

Transference of Trust
- The Art of Significant Selling

Making of a Champion
- The Art of
Significant Team Building

Speak Like a Pro
- The Art and Science of
Significant Public Speaking

Story Selling
– How to Persuade People to
Think, Feel, Act, Follow, Buy

The Art of Significant Network Marketing
(Audiobook and Study Guide)

Chicken Soup for the College Soul

The Most Popular Stories By Dan Clark in
Chicken Soup For The Soul

Puppies for Sale
(Illustrated Children's Hard Cover)

Slkkoul Food
(The Complete Dan Clark
Story Collection)

Dan Clark's Humor File
– A Repository of Jokes and B.S. Tales